MARINELLI COMPANIES

TECHNIQUES IN
COUNTERSURVEILLANCE

THE FINE ART OF BUG
EXTERMINATION IN
THE REAL WORLD OF
INTELLIGENCE GATHERING

PALADIN PRESS · BOULDER, COLORADO

Techniques in Countersurveillance:
The Fine Art of Bug Extermination
in the Real World of Intelligence Gathering
by Marinelli Companies

Copyright © 1999 by Marinelli Companies

ISBN 1-58160-020-8
Printed in the United States of America

Published by Paladin Press, a division of
Paladin Enterprises, Inc.
Gunbarrel Tech Center
7077 Winchester Circle
Boulder, Colorado 80301 USA
+1.303.443.7250

Direct inquiries and/or orders to the above address.

Visit our Web site at www.paladin-press.com

Contents

The Basics

Although surveillance means to keep a close watch over someone or something, a term more appropriate to our discussion is the archaic eavesdropping, which means to listen secretly to what is said in private, the term having derived from the practice of standing under the eaves and surreptitiously listening to a private conversation. Both of these terms describe a practice in widespread use these days, which is the gathering of information from a subject without the subject's knowledge. Probably the most well-known examples of this are practiced by government and law-enforcement agencies by their bugging a room, tapping a phone, or otherwise intercepting private communications, all to gather evidence for intelligence purposes or for prosecution. Almost as frequent are examples of corporate spying, such as bugging the competition to learn of new product lines, technical innovations, or upcoming stock manipulations. Mailing lists, patent infor-

▲

mation or formulas, financial reports, and the like all can give a competitor a distinct advantage.

Another major segment of the surveillance market involves domestic and private concerns. Divorce cases, child custody disputes, and small-business security (shoplifting, employee theft, and so on) are the grist that keeps many private investigation firms in business (a heavily disputed divorce case can generate more legal maneuvering and attempts to gather incriminating evidence than the most publicized Mafia prosecution).

There are numerous methods by which the bugger can obtain information from the buggee, and the acceleration of electronic technology has widened one's options significantly in the past two decades. The simplest approach involves a hard-wired microphone/recorder combination, several common systems for which are relatively easy to implement. For example, a small, discreet microphone may be hidden on the target premises and connected by a pair of wires to a remote recording device. Alternately, a microphone may be connected to a circuit that modulates the signal onto a 110-volt AC wiring network. (Similar to the wireless intercom systems widely available, this allows an operative to retrieve the signal from any outlet served by the same AC power network.)

A third method involves employing unused telephone cables. Many locations, especially businesses, have a multiple-conductor telephone cable entering the premises. Attaching a microphone and suitable preamp to an unused pair of cables allows one to monitor conversations from any point at which access to the phone wiring exists. Suitable filters are available to prevent "hum" pickup from adjacent AC wiring.

Obviously, hard-wired systems take time to install and require a period of uninterrupted access to the site. However, if properly installed with carefully concealed microphones and wiring, they are extremely difficult to detect because there is no radiated signal.

Microphones may be contact affairs, which are usually

▲

mounted in a wall on the opposite side of the room being monitored and pick up sound from the vibrations of the wall. They may also be "spike mikes," which are extremely small microphones built into the end of devices that resemble large nails; such a device can be driven into a wall from the opposite side and will remain virtually invisible from the target side. Most situations employ electret mikes, which are extremely small and very sensitive, with typical units being the size of a pencil eraser. They require a small amount of DC voltage to operate, but this can be applied from the receiving end of the interconnecting cable.

One case we were used in involved a miniature microphone and preamp hidden inside a telephone outlet box and wired to an unused pair of phone cables. The recorder was four floors below in the utility room, where the main telephone exchange was mounted. Disguised as a fuse box, it recorded everything said in the target site. The operator merely showed up periodically to change tapes. Once again, these systems may be hard to install, but properly done, they are extremely difficult to detect.

The most common method of bugging a room undoubtedly involves the use of radio-frequency-transmitting devices. A miniature transmitter with an attached microphone can be hidden almost anywhere. Transmitters have been disguised as fountain pens, cigarette packs, picture frames, plants, emergency lights, smoke detectors, and even an olive in a martini glass (the swizzle stick was the antenna). [1] Winston Arrington, in his excellent book Now Hear This [2], describes a vaginal transmitter; similar to a tampon, it was used at a topless beach to monitor conversations and was obviously well concealed. This is perhaps an extreme example of another category of radio frequency (RF) bugs—the body wire, one of the more common examples of which involves the police secreting a small transmitter somewhere on the body of an undercover agent before he goes out to make a drug buy.

The advantage of these devices is their ease of deployment. In many cases, simply placing an innocuous-appearing object at the target site allows monitoring of conversations from distances of several hundred feet to several miles. The major disadvantage is that these devices transmit on a radio frequency; anyone listening on that particular frequency can hear the same information the operator is monitoring. Problems can also arise because of battery failure.

All of these radio-frequency techniques work equally well with miniature video cameras; a hidden camera connected to a transmitter can send pictures as well as voice to a remote recording location.

Another broad category of surveillance techniques involves telephone bugs and taps. Bugging a phone generally means attaching an RF transmitter to the unit, whereas tapping a phone refers to attaching wires to the phone lines and running them to a remote monitoring or recording post. The terms are often used interchangeably.

Tapping phone lines and taping phone conversations or installing transmitting bugs have become so commonplace that the federal government has instituted laws and regulations regarding the use of such devices (see Appendix A). However, the ease with which these devices may be implemented often overcomes legal considerations on the theory that you're only guilty if you're caught. Given the widespread coverage of the telephone network, surveillance from a remote location is easily possible. Also, the interception of fax and computer-generated information has become so prevalent that security considerations are increasing. A steadily rising number of companies routinely send sensitive documents over the phone lines via fax, blissfully unaware of how easy it is to tap into the line at any point with another fax machine and intercept everything that's being transmitted with virtually no chance of detection. Issue No. 23 of *Full Disclosure* covers this topic at some length. [3]

Phone bugs may also transmit both sides of the phone conversation through the air just like an RF room transmitter

▲

(they sometimes use part of the phone wiring as an antenna). There are even units that transmit the phone conversation when the phone is in use and then become room-monitoring transmitters when the phone is hung up. [4]

Of course, one of the simplest methods of bugging a site merely involves hiding a tape recorder on the premises (usually with some form of voice-activation to conserve tape and battery life) and retrieving it at a later date. This also works with cameras and video recorders, a prime example being the "video briefcase," which is a video cassette recorder and camera with a suitable battery pack enclosed in a standard briefcase. Pinhole camera lenses are available that can peer through a hole in the case as small as an eighth of an inch in diameter and still cover extremely wide fields of view.

There are other, more exotic methods of surveillance available to the operative with both the necessary operating skills and an adequate budget.

Infrared transmitter/receiver combinations work on many of the same principles as radio-frequency devices, but they transmit the information via an invisible infrared light beam rather than radio waves. Although this requires the transmitter and receiver to be on a line-of-sight path, there is no radio signal emitted and standard RF sweep techniques do not work.

Even more elaborate are optical systems such as the laser beam reflector, which works because whenever a conversation takes place inside a room, the sound causes surfaces such as windows to vibrate, however minutely, in synchronization with the speech. If an invisible laser beam is aimed at the outside of the window from some remote location, some of the beam will be reflected back by the glass surface and will be modulated by the window's vibrations. A carefully placed detector can intercept this modulated beam and convert it to an exact replica of the conversation taking place inside the room. Although this requires extremely precise aiming, it is a very difficult system to detect.

Although all of these methods are illegal under one or more federal statutes, the possible benefits to the user generally far outweigh the potential penalties imposed, even in the unlikely event the user is apprehended and successfully prosecuted (Richard Nixon might disagree here). Of course, the feds are only guilty if they failed to enact legislation legalizing their tactics. All of the practices prohibited for the public by Title 3 are available to state and federal law-enforcement agencies, although even they must sometimes obtain court approval before implementing them.

Many corporations feel they have no choice but to spy on the competition, this because a surprise technical or tactical innovation can be a matter of life or death in the business world. Catching a soon-to-be ex-spouse in a compromising position can mean major differences in alimony or property settlements, and child custody disputes can generate emotional states that make legal considerations a moot point. Insider stock-trading information, details of planned mergers, impending real estate deals, and access to other privileged information can mean tremendous financial gain for one with advance notice.

The possibility of invasion of one's public or private affairs is so pervasive that security measures have taken on an importance bordering on hysteria. Security firms are turning away business and private countersurveillance consultants are in high demand.

Obviously, because of the numerous surveillance methods available to the bugger, the countersurveillance expert must possess a wide range of knowledge and the proper tools and diagnostic equipment, and must have a precise procedure to apply when searching a premises. Assuring a client that his site is clean only to find out later that there was a hidden bug you missed can ruin your professional reputation in short order.

In the coming chapters we'll take you through the process step by step, including the physical inspection, RF sweep, phone line security analysis, and much more. We'll explain what tools are necessary or useful and show you how to use them. Construction details for several useful pieces of test equipment are outlined and a list of suppliers of commercial units is included. Excerpts from appropriate federal regulations are reprinted and a bibliography of pertinent publications follows.

ENDNOTES

1. Holt, Patricia. *Bug In The Martini Olive and Other True Cases from the Files of Hal Lipset, Private Eye*. New York: Little, Brown and Co., 1991.

2. Arrington, Winston. *Now Hear This*. Chicago: Sheffield Electronics, 1988. An excellent book on the design and construction of bugs and telephone surveillance equipment

3. *Full Disclosure*. Attn: Glen Roberts, Box 1533, Oil City, PA 16301

4. Sheffield Electronics Model TEL-115K. 7223 Stony Island Ave., Chicago, Illinois 60649. Sheffield provides kits for surveillance transmitters of exceptional quality and value.

The Physical Inspection

As an example of how a countersurveillance investigation is conducted, let's go through a typical situation from start to finish. We'll be using a commercial business site as an example, but everything covered would apply to a private residence as well. For brevity we'll call the entire process of physical inspection, RF inspection, phone line security analysis, and so on a "sweep."

Assuming you (the sweeper) and the client have arrived at a contractual agreement (it is difficult to imagine a situation where one would agree to do a sweep without some kind of legal contract), the first step is to determine the scope of the investigation. Some clients may only wish to have their phone lines vetted to make sure they're "clean." Others may want a full-fledged sweep of the entire building. Obviously, some degree of common sense comes into play here and you must put yourself on the other side of the fence and ask "If I want-ed to bug this place, what would be the easiest and most effective method? What would be the easiest way to gain access? What kind of information do I wish to obtain? How much is that information worth to my client and how much time and expense do I want to expend to get it?" (Keep in mind that most bugs are as difficult to retrieve as they are to plant; they are usually left in place and written off as a fixed expense.) For a simple divorce case (if there is such a thing), it's highly unlikely that sophisticated laser techniques and the like would be employed. On the other hand, the research and development branch of a major corporation might be well advised to have every possibility investigated.

Another service complementary to the actual sweep involves installing electronic countermeasures (ECM) equipment, which are devices intended to disable, mask, jam, or otherwise render ineffective any surveillance gear already in place. There is also the matter of evaluating existing security and burglar alarm systems and instituting training programs for the staff in security and countersurveillance considerations. (These areas will be covered in a separate chapter along with on-going programs of periodic re-inspections.) The scope of services to be performed should be clearly spelled out in the contract in advance.

The next decision is whether the sweep should be a covert operation, for to warn your enemy that he's been discovered is to give him yet another weapon. If the bugger becomes aware that his target premises is undergoing a sweep, he has several options. For example, many transmitters are duplex affairs, meaning that they can be shut down from the listening post with a simple radio command. This totally defeats the sweep process—you can't find it if it isn't operating. Alternatively, the bugger might just wait until the sweep is completed and then plant another bug.

Sometimes the client doesn't care if the bugger knows his devices are being hunted for, and on occasion time is so critical that discretion must be sacrificed. If the board meeting starts in one hour and the chairman is paranoid about the possibility of a compromised room, a covert operation is almost impossible.

Another possibility worth consideration is the option of disinformation. If a client knows he is being monitored, he may wish to discuss matters of a false or misleading nature to purposely confuse the information gatherer. This can also provide a means of identifying the bugger; providing a critical piece of data to the surveillance system, anyone later displaying a knowledge of this "tagged" information becomes a suspect.

In most cases, however, a discreet, covert operation is in order. This generally involves conducting the sweep when the staff is away (there's always the possibility the bugging was an inside job). Usual procedures involve night sweeps when the business is closed, which eliminates having to answer lots of questions and keeps unnecessary people out of your way.

It's generally most effective to have at least two people on the sweep team. Three or four are best because a complete sweep is quite time consuming, and any larger force makes it difficult to camouflage the operation. Many operatives employ disguises on the theory the building may be under visual surveillance as well, and a troop of technicians lugging anvil cases full of test gear through the front door late at night is highly suspect. One of the better firms we've seen dresses their operatives in coveralls and arrives in a van marked as a janitorial service. A large dolly similar to those used by cleaning crews and festooned with mops and brooms hides the equipment and makes it easy to wheel everything right through the door.

Once inside, normal conversation about cleaning functions or whatever is appropriate, but a set of code words or hand signals should be devised to communicate anything relating to the sweep. Even if the bugger's listening post is shut down for the night, any voice-operated tape machines will still function, and if the bugger listens to the tape the next day and hears one of your guys shout "Hey, come check this out. I think I've found one!," the bugger will have a pretty good idea of what went on.

▲

It also helps to have a floor plan of the entire building in advance and to have assigned tasks to the various team members so that, once inside the building, the sweep can commence with a minimum amount of confusion and wasted time. As the search proceeds, suspicious or vulnerable areas should be indicated on the diagram.

More bugs are probably found during a thorough physical search than by all other techniques combined. It's also about the only way to find hard-wired mikes and hidden tape recorders. The first thing to do is visually check for any signs of hidden cameras, because if there are any in operation, the bugger will know immediately what you're up to. Unfortunately, any bugger worth his pay will have concealed them so well that they will take quite a bit of ferreting out to locate. Besides, if they are obvious enough for you to see them, the client will probably have spotted them himself.

Some sweepers will check for video transmissions on all the common bands from outside the building before they even enter. If there are no unusual signals present, they can be relatively certain that no video transmitters are in operation. However, it is still possible for a video transmitter to be present in a dormant state, waiting to be triggered by a motion sensor. If video transmissions are present, these transmissions can then be effectively jammed, but this will also alert the bugger of an impending search.

It's less likely you will pick up audio transmissions from an RF bug while outside the building because most of these units are voice-operated to conserve battery life (and to prevent you from doing just what we're talking about). Common audio frequencies can be checked en masse with a spectrum analyzer and whip antenna. Any strong local signal's amplitude will stand out quite noticeably. More about this when we get into RF sweeping.

Once the team is inside and the equipment is unpacked, the members go about their various tasks. One group is assigned the job of checking all likely hiding places on the walls and floor, which typically involves removing covers from AC outlets, TV outlets, thermostat housings, and any other wall covering that might conceal a bug. They pay particular attention to AC outlets because many transmitters are mounted in or near them to gain access to the 110-volt wiring for their power source, thereby eliminating the hassles common to battery-powered units. Heating and air-conditioning duct covers are also possibilities but are rarely used because, if they are in operation, the noise of the moving air will mask anything the mike might pick up.

Another group checks light fixtures, smoke detectors, and so on, and if there is a drop ceiling, removes sections to check for anything hidden above them. One popular video camera mount is disguised as a ceiling sprinkler system. The camera is mounted above and has a pinhole lens that looks down through the sprinkler nozzle, which has a tiny mirror mounted at 45 degrees to permit a horizontal field of view.

It's virtually impossible to list all the places a transmitter may be hidden, such as hollowed out books, VCR cassettes, clocks, table lamps, and filing cabinets, to name a few. Anything that could possibly hide a bug, no matter how remote that possibility might seem, should be investigated.

Another step is checking telephones. On a standard handset, the covers over the mouthpiece and earpiece can be unscrewed (an oil filter wrench is handy for this purpose). The elements will drop out and any bugs should be visible. A common method of quickly planting a bug uses "drop-in" transmitters, which are bugs built into the back of a microphone element identical to the ones used in standard pho   The operative simply unscrews the mouthpiece cover ar   ele-ments. Although the range is fairly limited (ap feet), this is an extremely quick method of de

Popping the cover off the base of the ' easy and should reveal any internal bugs ups. If the phone plugs into the wall w unplug it before doing these checks s

▲

will not be picked up by any line taps. Don't forget the covers over the terminal boxes and modular jacks, and be sure to check any answering machines as well. If there is a fax machine or computer modem attached, a thorough physical inspection is in order.

Another point worth mentioning here is that if you locate a bug, don't pack it up and start making out the bill. Any surveillance job worth the fees most operatives charge dictates several back-up units. We've heard of commercial offices with several phone taps, a couple of RF transmitters, and a hidden tape recorder to boot. A standard trick with phone taps is to install one fairly obvious unit with a secondary device much more deeply hidden. The sweeper finds the first tap and shouts "Eureka!," assuming the phone is now sanitized, and then completely overlooks the second transmitter. The more critical the application, the higher the likelihood of multi-layer devices.

As we've said, a physical inspection is about the only method available to find hard-wired systems. An operative will generally prefer to use existing wiring to get his signal to the outside world, where it can be taped or transmitted. The most common approaches use phone lines, intercom wiring, burglar alarm wiring, and cable or antenna television distribution systems. Intercom stations and burglar alarm sensors should be inspected carefully for any signs of tampering. A scope is handy here. More later.

One common method of sending a video signal from a hidden camera involves modulating, or mixing, this signal onto existing television cabling, often as an upper UHF channel. The signal propagates along the coaxial cable right along with the legitimate signals. All the bugger has to do is tap into another outlet served by the same source (antenna or cable feed) and tune in his signal. This is especially common in structures such as motels and apartment buildings where all rooms share a common signal source. You should have a le TV, preferably one with manual tuning on both VHF and UHF. Attach it to an outlet and dial from below channel 2 to above channel 83, watching for any bogus signals. A spectrum analyzer is handy for this task as well (see Chapter 4).

Hidden audio and video recorders are also best located with a physical inspection. Although there are units that will detect the minute amount of radiation thrown off by the recorder's bias oscillator circuitry, they need to be extremely close to register anything, and proper shielding of the recorder will prevent even that. Again, the maxim is if in doubt, take it apart.

Only experience can tell you how much time to spend on the physical inspection before moving on to the more active phases of RF sweeping and live-phone-line analysis. If the room is an office with lots of equipment and furniture, a thorough physical inspection can take all night. Conversely, a conference room, with minimal furniture and fixtures, can be analyzed in short order.

When in doubt, move on to the next phase. If you detect unusual transmissions or radiations, you can generally zero in on them enough to narrow the area of search.

Next comes the fun part: checking the electromagnetic spectrum from DC to daylight to look for active radiating sources. (The electromagnetic spectrum consists of varying wavelengths, one of which is a DC wavelength. Another is a sinusoidal wave of daylight.)

RF Transmitter Bugs

In this chapter we'll discuss bugs that transmit on radio frequencies. To effectively search for them, it's necessary to know how they operate and which frequencies they commonly use.

The electromagnetic spectrum is measured in cycles per second, which is the number of times the electromagnetic field changes polarity. Cycles per second is now commonly referred to as Hertz, in honor of Heinrich Hertz (no relationship to the car rental company), a 19th century German physicist who applied theories to the production and reception of radio waves. Somehow, cycles per second still seems more descriptive. However, we'll use the standard nomenclature Hertz.

Those audio frequencies to which the human ear responds range from 20 Hertz to 20,000 Hertz. Common abbreviations are "kilo" to represent 1,000 and Hz as shorthand for Hertz. This range of 20 Hz to 20 kiloHertz (kHz) is

▲

the range that the microphones employed in surveillance gear pick up.

In practice, the pick-up range or "frequency response" of these microphones and transmitters is often limited to a range from about 200 Hz to 3,000 Hz (3 kHz). This is often referred to as "Ma Bell" frequency response because the phone company found that this range contained all the fundamental frequencies of the human voice. Multiples of these fundamental frequencies, called harmonics, add subtle shadings and colorations to the basic tones and allow one to distinguish between, say, a piccolo and a flute, but this subtlety is unnecessary for intelligent recognition of voice communications. Neither the surveillance man nor the phone company is interested in transmitting studio-quality high fidelity, especially since it takes more bandwidth—and hence more power—to accommodate the wider frequency response. This technique also eliminates unnecessary sensitivity to low frequency pickup, such as 60 Hz power-line hum, and high-frequency noise (amplifier hiss).

Once we get above the audio range, we start dealing with what are known as radio frequencies. These are frequencies which, when traveling down a wire, radiate a signal into space. This is precisely the principle on which antennas operate.

There are acronyms for various groups of frequencies, such as VLF (very low frequency of several hundred kHz or so), VHF (very high frequency of 30 to 300 MHz), UHF (ultra-high frequency of 300 to 1,000 MHz), and so on. (See Appendix D for a chart of frequency allocations used for various services and note the vastly differing bandwidth required by different types of transmissions.)

A voice transmitter essentially takes an input signal, in this case the signal from the microphone, and impresses it on or modulates a higher frequency signal, known as the carrier frequency. In the amplitude modulation (AM) mode, the audio frequencies are used to change the magnitude (amplitude) of the carrier frequency. In the FM mode (frequency

▲

modulation), the audio information is used to change the frequency of the carrier up or down by a small amount (known as deviation). The receiver senses these slight variations in the frequency of the carrier and converts this information into a replica of the original audio modulating signal (see Appendix D). These carrier frequencies range from a few hundred kHz up to several billion Hz. A million Hz is abbreviated MHz for megaHertz and a billion Hz (1,000 MI-Lz) is referred to as a gigaHertz or GHz. FM is generally the only practical modulation method for surveillance transmitters. AM is considerably less efficient and is subject to noise and interference, whereas single sideband (SSB) techniques require a considerably more complex transmitter design, which increases size to an unacceptable degree.

There has been some recent use of digital and pulsed-signal transmission similar to the way a computer would send a signal over the phone lines (see Appendix D), which has the advantage of being indecipherable to anyone without the proper decoding unit, but size and complexity again become problems. This technique is rarely used outside the federal sphere. However, most remote control transmissions, such as garage door openers and radio control signals for model airplanes, are digital. These signals generally have to convey a limited amount of information, usually a variety of command codes to turn devices on and off. Voice communications using this method are a vastly more complex task. The new compact discs (CDs) and digital audio tape (DAT), as used in high-fidelity sound systems, sample the audio frequency of the sound rapidly and convert the instantaneous frequency to a train of pulses. On replay, the unit reconverts these pulsed signals into an analog audio signal nearly identical to the original. To maintain fidelity, however, the sampling process must occur at an extremely rapid rate, which results in a very complex coded signal. The circuitry necessary to accomplish this is much too cumbersome for most covert applications.

EFFICIENCY AND PROPAGATION

It's important to have an understanding of where various services are located in the spectrum, and also how signals travel (propagate) at these frequencies. Lower frequencies, which have longer wavelengths, tend to follow the curvature of the earth and penetrate intervening structures more easily than higher frequencies with their shorter wavelengths, which travel a straight path (line-of-sight) but are more easily absorbed (attenuated) by any obstacle.

One other factor: any transmitter will work most efficiently or deliver it's maximum power output capability into an antenna that is some sub-multiple of its wavelength. Most common antennas are either one quarter or one half of the wavelength of the frequency the transmitter is operating at. A one-half wave antenna for 30 MHz is approximately 16 feet long, whereas at microwave frequencies we're talking several inches or less (see Appendix D).

Both the propagation characteristics and the antenna length set some limits as to the frequencies available for practical transmission from a surveillance transmitter. There's also the matter of efficiency—how much power does the transmitter consume versus how much power it radiates from its antenna? This becomes a critical factor for battery-operated transmitters. More on this in the appendices (see power formula and battery table in Appendix C).

From much experimenting in the field and theoretical considerations, it has been found that the optimum performance from a bug will occur somewhere in a band from about 30 MHz to 500 MHz or so. Below this range, efficiency, antenna length, and transmitter size become problems, while above it, propagation problems and attenuation limit their usefulness. There are some microwave bugs in use, but the line-of-sight requirements limit them to special situations only. Low-frequency transmitters (30 to 500 kHz) are primarily used for marine applications. These applications typically require extremely long antennas (several hundred feet) but give extremely long range, especially for voice or code applications.

COMMONLY USED FREQUENCIES

Probably the most common frequencies used lie in or near the commercial FM band. A glance through any electronics magazine will reveal an incredible number of companies offering "FM Wireless Mike" kits. Designed to broadcast your own voice through your own FM radio, they are rarely, if ever, used for this purpose (see Chapter 4). By selling them as kits, the companies circumvent the FCC prohibition against sale or shipment of surveillance transmitters to the public. They are not considered RF interception devices until they are assembled, and the average surveillance operator has a box full of them. They're also easy to monitor; any reasonably sensitive FM receiver will suffice. Unfortunately, they are also the least secure because anyone within range with an FM radio who happens to tune across the same frequency will also hear the monitored conversation. There's no point in doing a covert surveillance if everyone else in town is listening in. This also increases the likelihood of the target picking up his own signal. If the buggee is tuning his FM receiver and hits the same frequency as a transmitter operating nearby, a feedback situation occurs, usually a high-pitched whine identical to the squeal you hear at concerts when the musicians turn their amplifiers up too high and the sound gets back into the mike. It goes round and round, starting out as a low-pitched rumble and ending up as a screech.

Obviously, the surveillance operative would like to have his bug operate on a vacant frequency as far from commercial services as possible. Unfortunately, space in the spectrum is at a premium and it's almost all in use for one purpose or another.

Another problem is the availability of commercially manufactured transmitters. Most companies who make these units will sell only to federal agencies or law-enforcement groups because they can get into serious difficulties for selling to the general public.

One exception to this exists in the two commercial business bands. These bands are designed for two-way communications for businesses such as cab companies, delivery services, and so on. Technically, to operate on these bands one must apply to the FCC for a license and be granted a specific

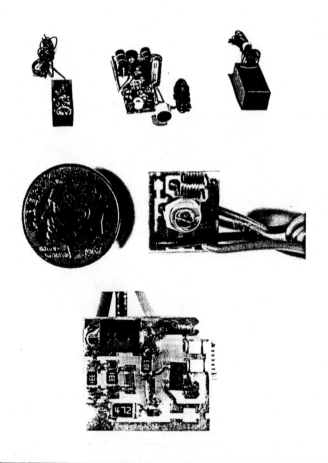

Radio frequency transmitters.

frequency for his own private use. (Generally, no one else within a 60-mile radius is granted the same channel.)

It is the responsibility of the purchaser to apply for and obtain a license, but there is widespread abuse of this requirement. The lower band runs from 150 MHz to 170 MHz, but the upper half (above about 160 MHz) is used by many police and law-enforcement groups and is studiously avoided by any intelligent surveillance types (see Appendix D). The other band starts at 450 MHz and is less densely populated than the 150 MHz band. Even though this band has a lot of activity, especially in a densely crowded urban area, the availability of off-the-shelf gear often offers the only choice for an operative who is unwilling or unable to build his own transmitters or modify existing products.

Theoretically, a surveillance agent could apply for a business license and have his own frequency assigned, but eavesdropping is an invasion of privacy and is not considered a legitimate business. Quite the contrary, because intentionally intercepting transmissions is a criminal act, the operative would not want an intercepted surveillance transmission to be traced to him simply by someone looking up who's licensed for that frequency. Hence, most use of these bands is rather clandestine. In small towns and rural areas, where band activity is sparse, chances of interception decrease proportionately.

The 450 MHz band has been gaining popularity because it requires shorter antennas and is more immune to interference because of the relative inactivity. However, it does have more problems with line-of-sight propagation characteristics.

There are two other major advantages to this gear. First, the transmitters are usually crystal controlled. That means their operating frequency is fixed and maintained by means of a precisely ground quartz crystal, which eliminates the transmitter's drifting off frequency. All FM wireless mikes, for example, use a tunable, uncontrolled oscillator to set their operating frequency. Changes in temperature, aging batteries, and movement of the unit all can cause the signal to drift

▲

away from its original frequency. If you're continually monitoring the receiver, this can be corrected by slight retuning of the receiver. However, unattended recording becomes a real problem because it doesn't take much of a frequency change before the receiver loses its ability to lock onto the signal.

The other major advantage has to do with the receiver. Most receiving units designed for these signals have what is known as adjustable squelch. This is a circuit that turns off or mutes the output of the receiver when there is no actual modulated signal, and only gives an audio output when a sufficiently strong signal is being received, i.e., whenever there are voices being transmitted. This makes connection to a tape recorder with voice-activated turn-on much simpler (see Appendix C).

One final topic here before we discuss actually locating these devices. A bug is, by its very nature, a small, low-power transmitter that is small for ease of concealment and deployment; and low power not only to conserve battery life (if batteries are the power source) but also because the monitoring station is usually in the vicinity and there is a distinct liability in having the signal propagate any farther than necessary. This would increase the likelihood of someone else intercepting the transmission. Nonetheless, because you will be very close to it when you're hunting for it, the bug will still sound like one of the strongest signals on the dial.

Now to the hunt.

RF Transmitter
Sweeping Receivers

To do a successful RF sweep, several pieces of equipment are necessary. At the top of the list is a sensitive FM receiver that will cover from 20 or 30 MHz to at least 500 MHz with no gaps. Although hand-held scanners will suffice, they are difficult to fine tune. A general coverage communications receiver with manual tuning is a much better choice.

Battery operation is also desirable because you'll be moving it around quite a bit. Additional features should include selectable bandwidth (wide band/narrow band FM modes), adjustable squelch threshold, a headphone jack that disables the built-in speaker, and a reliable and sensitive signal-strength meter.

Yaesu, ICOM, AR, Panasonic, Kenwood, Sony, and others all make general coverage communications receivers designed to operate off 12 volts, such as a car's electrical system, which meet the above requirements. We use a Yaesu general coverage receiver with a short telescoping whip antenna. It's about the size of a cigar box and we hang it from a neck strap for easy portability. It has a 12-volt input jack on the rear panel, and we carry several 12-volt rechargeable Gel-Cells in ammo pouches worn on a web belt (available from your local army surplus store). Spare batteries are highly recommended because the primary one usually dies just before the job is finished.

Two other items complement the receiver package: a cassette deck or boom box with a tape of elevator music or some other innocuous-sounding tunes that might be played as background music in many buildings, and a good set of headphones.

The purpose of the cassette system is to generate sounds for the bug(s) to pick up, which will hopefully be quite innocent to the surveillance monitor but which you can identify when you tune the signal in on your receiver. Many bugs require an incoming signal from the mike (VOX or voice-operated relay) before they power up and start transmitting.

The headphones are necessary to prevent feedback loops from occurring when you hit the bug's transmission signal. If you were to use the built-in speaker, it would reproduce the same signal the bug was hearing and transmitting, resulting in a feedback situation such as we described in Chapter 3. This is a dead giveaway to the monitor that a sweep is in progress. A good set of phones, preferably the surround or earmuff type, are invaluable—they cut out background noise and eliminate distraction. A mixer can be incorporated to feed signals from your associates' walkie talkies if desired (see Appendix C).

The usual procedure is to play the tape at moderate levels in the room under test and, while listening through the headphones, slowly tune the receiver from one end of its frequency range to the other. If there is an active bug in the room you'll hear your own tape when you hit the frequency on which the bug is transmitting. Once you've locked in on the signal, moving around with the receiver while watching the signal strength meter should help pinpoint the location of the bug. A receiver with a front-end sensitivity control (RF gain control) or input attenuator is handy to prevent receiver overload when you get very close to the transmitter (see Appendix C).

At this point, it pays to keep in mind what we discussed in the previous chapter concerning the most often used bands and commonly available equipment. The commercial FM broadcast band merits special attention, especially in domestic cases or any other situation where the bugger might tend to be less sophisticated than, say, in a major corporate case.

Many surveillance types realign their FM receiver to extend its coverage slightly above or below the normal band limits of 88-108 MHz. One should be particularly alert for signals from 82 MHz to 112 MHz. This is about as far as a commercial receiver can be detuned.

Another nasty trick eavesdroppers use is to hide their signal "on the shoulder" of a strong local FM station. This means they tune their transmitter as close as possible to a powerful commercial station, which makes it easier to miss when tuning across the band. It also makes it less likely to be noticed on a spectrum analyzer display, which we'll get to shortly.

The same theories apply in the business bands, from 150 to 170 MHz and 450 to about 470 MHz. On these bands the receiver should be set to the narrow-bandwidth mode because the signals are likely to be crystal controlled with very little frequency deviation.

An extremely crude surveillance methods involve buying a pair of citizen's band walkie-talkies and taping down the push-to-talk button on the one that's hidden at the site. It pays to check these CB channels located at and above 27 MHz. There's also some activity between 45 and 49 MHz, where a lot of commercially available remote-control equipment can be modified. The same is true up around 330 MHz (garage door openers, Medic-Alert, and so on).

There are also several amateur radio bands spread throughout the range we've been discussing, and equipment is readily available off the shelf. However, "hams" monitor their frequencies like hawks and the possibility of getting away with a clandestine transmission on one of their bands is highly unlikely. The one exception to this is the two-meter band from 142 to 149 MHz. This is by far the most popular ham band for short-range communication using pocket-size transceivers (transmitter/receiver combinations), and in a remote rural area with light amateur activity, a unit that is turned down in power to cover just a few hundred feet could easily go undetected.

These are just some of the more common frequencies used. One should diligently check every frequency from end to end of the receiver's range because a good operative will build or modify a transmitter to work on a frequency where activity would be least expected. Remember that an infestation can occur anywhere.

RF SNIFFERS

Although a successful RF sweep could be carried out with only the aforementioned equipment, there are several additional devices that greatly simplify the task. The most useful of these is undoubtedly the RF "sniffer." This is a hand-held untuned receiver with a short whip antenna and a signal strength meter. Because there are no tuning circuits in the front end of the receiver, it simultaneously picks up all signals at any frequency within its bandwidth. Typical units operate from 100 kHz or so all the way up to a gigaHertz. The readout indicates the sum of the signal strengths of every signal received. Although at first glance this may seem like a useless idea, with all of the TV stations, FM stations, commercial transmissions, and so on in the air at the same time, the addition of a sensitivity control completely changes the picture.

In actual use, the sensitivity control is adjusted so that the combined signal strengths just start to deflect the readout upwards. Then, if the unit is moved closer to a transmitting bug, the readout moves upscale. The closer the bug, the higher the reading.

▲

One of the characteristics of electromagnetic radiation is that the signal strength decreases relative to the square of the distance traveled. In other words, if you take a reading of signal strength at a given distance from the source, at twice that distance you get one fourth the reading, at three times the distance, you get one ninth the original level, and so on. This means that even if there's a 100,000-watt TV station a mile down the road, if you're one foot away from a one-watt bug, the signal from the bug will be considerably higher. This makes for a very useful bug detector. Being sensitive to virtually any frequency that a bug might be operating on, merely approaching the bug will cause an increasing readout. Some units use an audio tone that increases in pitch as signal strength increases and others use a bar graph display. Both will indicate the presence of a transmitter if brought close enough to the bug.

In practice, if the sensitivity is properly adjusted to just barely indicate the combined level of all the background signals, a noticeable increase in readout will occur when the unit is moved to a couple of feet away from the average power bug, and will increase dramatically as it is brought even closer.

In actual use, the device is passed over all wall surfaces, outlets, fixtures, and any other suspicious area. It essentially "sniffs" for the presence of radiation anywhere within its bandwidth. Needless to say, this can greatly speed up the sweep process. The units are quite small and inexpensive enough (in the $100 – $250 range) that each member of your team should have one. Commercial units have probes for infrared pickup, tape recorder oscillator circuits, and so on (see Appendix C). We also include circuit board layouts and construction details for a simple yet effective unit that you can build yourself.

OSCILLOSCOPES

Some transmitters, especially those wired into the AC line for their operating power, use that same AC line as an antenna. It's advisable and relatively easy to check for these with an oscilloscope, and it's best to use a battery-powered scope because of grounding and polarity considerations. (NonLinear Systems, B & K, and Tektronix all make small portable units.) Simply plug the probe into one side of the AC outlet and the ground lead into the other side and you should see a nice, clean sine wave. Check at various sweep speeds; if there is any signal riding on the 110-volt, 60-cycle AC wave, it will be easily seen (see Appendix D) This is also the best way to check for systems like wireless intercoms, which don't use the AC lines as an antenna but rather function as a wired carrier for the audio signal (these are known as carrier current devices). Oscilloscopes can also be handy for telephone line analysis, as we'll see later.

FREQUENCY COUNTERS

Another small, inexpensive, yet extremely useful piece of test gear is a frequency counter. Let's say that you've located a possible transmitting device during the physical search and you wish to monitor it. Instead of hunting all over the dial with your FM receiver to locate its frequency, you can employ a frequency counter to pinpoint its operating frequency within a few cycles per second.

These units are essentially event counters, which count the number of cycles of an AC wave over a preset time interval. They are usually crystal controlled and compute the frequency in terms of Hertz. They are usually equipped for surveillance work with a short whip antenna for pickup, and if within a few feet of the radiating source will display the frequency on a four- to eight-digit readout. Accuracy ranges from one part in 10 +6 to one part in 10 +9 for units with a temperature-controlled oven for the time-base crystal. This latter accuracy would give a readout accurate to one cycle at one GHz. There are also pre-scalers to extend the frequency coverage, and the relatively new development of active pre-selectors, which are extremely useful for countersurveillance work. See Appendix C for further information.

SPECTRUM ANALYZERS

One of the most highly regarded yet least understood pieces of test gear is the spectrum analyzer. In many sweepers' opinion, this is the ultimate diagnostic tool because having one automatically makes you an expert. Some operatives think the client will be impressed by the imposing array of knobs, dials, and readouts. Unfortunately, even among those fortunate enough to own one, very few know how to properly use it.

This device can monitor an entire band of frequencies simultaneously and display them in real time as a function of signal strength versus frequency. In its simplest format, this unit consists of three components: a tunable radio receiver, a sweep circuit that continuously and repetitively tunes the receiver from one end of the desired band to the other, and a display readout that shows relative signal strength and that is synchronized to the sweep circuitry. The display is typically an oscilloscope, which is a device with a cathode-ray tube (CRT) for a readout. An electron beam sweeps across its face from left to right and back to repeat at a rapid rate. Voltage applied to a vertical drive circuit deflects the beam upward from the baseline in an amount proportional to the magnitude of the voltage present.

If the vertical signal is derived from the output of the radio receiver and the receiver is tuned across a band of frequencies, every time a transmitted signal is received, the beam will deflect vertically, thus indicating the strength of the incoming signal.

The remaining circuit to complete the analyzer is the sweep circuit, which automatically tunes the receiver and also drives the CRT beam horizontally at the same rate. The resulting display represents the band of frequencies being observed with the lowest frequency at the left edge of the CRT baseline,

▲

with the highest on the right. At each frequency with an active transmission present there will be a vertical line corresponding to the strength of the transmission.

Three basic adjustments control the operation of the analyzer: a center-frequency adjustment, which sets the middle of the display to a given frequency; a sweep width control, which sets how far above and below the center frequency will be displayed on the CRT; and a sweep rate, which determines how fast the beam and tuning control will traverse the range of frequencies.

If such a circuit were connected to an FM receiver with the center frequency set at 98 MHz and the sweep width set at 20 MHz (from 10 MHz below center to 10 MHz above), the display would show the entire commercial FM broadcast band and indicate all active FM stations in the area simultaneously. It might look something like this.

All types of modulation formats are visible and the vertical scale can be calibrated to indicate relative signal strength.

If the sweep width is set very wide, the entire spectrum—from a few MHz to several hundred MHz—is displayed. As the width is decreased, the "window" looks at smaller and smaller segments of the spectrum. At the narrow end, a single transmission can be spread out across the entire width of the display. Looking at a TV station transmission in this manner reveals the picture carrier, the sound sub-carrier, and any additional sub-carriers individually.

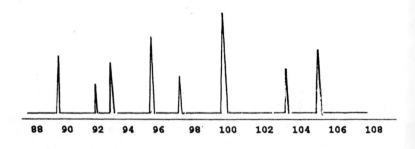

Pips.

Obviously, such a device would greatly simplify the task of searching for hidden transmitters. Even though they are usually quite low in power, if they are transmitting from a relatively close location their signal strength would be quite high relative to a distant commercial station.

Keep in mind, however, that the vertical line or "pip" produced by a surveillance transmitter will appear identical to a commercial station. Because the transmission is probably a frequency modulation mode, the height of the pip will not change with modulation. However, if you move about the room, a pip generated by a bug will change in height as you approach or recede from the location. The line from a commercial station a few miles away will not be affected by the slight change in relative distance if you move 10 feet farther away, but moving 10 feet closer to a bug that is 20 feet away will result in a noticeable increase in the amplitude of the marker.

Most analyzers have a manual tuning mode that disables the sweep circuitry and allows one to tune the unit like a standard receiver, this so that each pip may be tuned to center screen and listened to individually. Theoretically, you could investigate each pip to determine if it was a legitimate transmission, but then a standard communications receiver would suffice and the utility of the analyzer is lost.

One option available on the more expensive models of analyzers is a memory mode. This effectively stores a copy of whatever is appearing on the screen in a memory bank for later retrieval. There's a neat trick that can be used with this arrangement for bands of frequencies like the FM broadcast band. At a location remote from the search site (which you know to be free of bogus transmissions), a memory reading is taken of the entire band. This memory map can then be inverted, that is, the pips would now go below the base line, an exact upside-down copy of the original. This can then be algebraically added to a new readout of the same band and all the constant signals would be canceled out, resulting in a straight baseline with no pips. An inverted map is obtained at a clean location and is then added to the readout at the target site. If there is a spurious transmission at the site, then everything will be canceled out except for the bogus transmission, which will be the only marker visible. This works on bands like the commercial broadcast bands (where transmissions are constant) but is useless for bands like the business band, where signals are sporadic.

If you consistently do sweeps in the same geographical area, you soon start to recognize the legitimate transmissions and their relative amplitudes and acquire an ability to recognize suspicious markers.

Another use for spectrum analyzers involves the relatively new method of signal transmission known as frequency hopping. This is a technique whereby the transmitted signal is sent for a brief period (typically fractions of a second) on one frequency, then switched for another brief period to another frequency, and so on. The receiver has an identical list of frequencies stored in its memory and switches in synchronization with the transmitter so that it is always on the correct frequency to hear the transmitter. With the advent of frequency-synthesized local oscillators and scanner–receivers with 100-channel memory tuning, this has become quite easy to implement.

This is a very difficult type of transmission to pinpoint because the signal never stays put on a fixed frequency long enough to zero in on. With an analyzer, however, it will be quite apparent. There will be a pip that appears to jump all over the readout in a random manner. After a number of jumps the pattern will repeat itself. As many as 16 different frequencies are typically used before the sequence repeats.

Another clever method of transmitting information to avoid detection is called "burst" transmission. In this case, signals received at the target site are stored in some form of memory and then transmitted all at once. The storage device works like a voice-operated tape deck in that all dead time between actual conversations is eliminated so that a steady, condensed stream of data is available for transmission whenever needed.

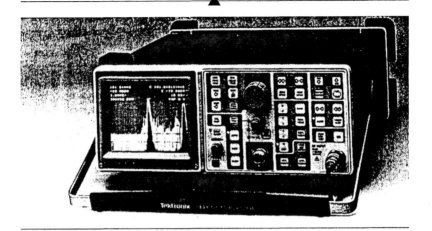

The Tektronix 2710 spectrum analyzer.

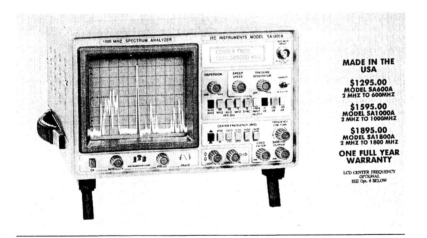

ITC's 1800 MHz spectrum analyzer.

These transmissions can be triggered by a preset timer, usually at a time when monitoring by sweepers would be least likely or it may be triggered via remote control from a listening post. For example, a room pick-up mike feeding a memory unit and transmitter would store all conversations for, say, 24 hours, eliminating all dead time in between. If this arrangement were connected to a radio-controlled activator, an operative could drive by the target site at 4:00 AM and trigger the affair. It would dump all the data via its transmitter and then go back to the off-the-air data-gathering mode until triggered again. One clever arrangement we've heard of uses the new AT&T digital telephone answering machine, which has fantastic memory capability, is quite small, and can apparently be easily modified.

It should be noted that spectrum analyzers are not inexpensive, with commercial models ranging from $3,000 to more than $10,000. Some of the more popular models are listed in the appendices. There are also kits available for considerably less for those willing to do a bit of home-brew construction. [1]

SUBCARRIER TRANSMISSION

Another sophisticated technique used by the surveillance operative is subcarrier transmission or FM/FM modulation. This involves using the audio information to frequency modulate a relatively low-frequency carrier, usually below 100 kHz. This carrier is in turn used to modulate a higher frequency carrier on the desired operating frequency. The lower frequency carrier is then referred to as the "subcarrier." This method is commonly used by commercial FM stations to transmit background music for businesses and offices along with their standard broadcast programming. It requires a separate decoder or demodulator to be attached to the output of the receiver's main demodulator section. Anyone tuning in the main carrier cannot hear the subcarrier transmissions. The advantage of this process for surveillance use is obvious and detection is almost impossible without knowing the subcarrier frequency. A spectrum analyzer will show all subcarriers, however, and once located, they can be analyzed by standard techniques.

See the appendices for specialized units that detect and identify subcarrier transmissions. There are also construction plans for a subcarrier tuner.

▲

AUTOMATED SWEEPS

Another countersurveillance technique that's gaining popularity involves automated sweeps. This involves creating a sound in the target room that is coded or otherwise unique, which can be recognized by a decoding device attached to the receiver. The receiver is tuned, or scans, the RF spectrum from end to end in much the same fashion as a spectrum analyzer and tries to find a transmission of this coded signal. When the high end of the band is reached, the process repeats itself. If a match is found, the time and frequency of the transmission is recorded and the search continues. This permits full-time, unattended monitoring of a site. One currently available unit [2] uses a series of three touch-tone signals identical to the dial tones used in telephone systems and plays these in a repeating pattern through a small amplifier and speaker in the target room. A touch-tone decoder attached to the receiver looks for a transmission of these same tones from a hidden bug as the receiver slowly scans the band. When a match is found, an attached cassette deck records the time and frequency. This is a handy way of continuously checking for the presence of bugs, especially duplex or timer-activated systems that may not be active full time.

RADIO DIRECTION FINDERS

One last piece of test gear that's useful, especially in large areas or buildings is the radio direction finder, or RDF. If you're sweeping a relatively small office or conference room and you detect a spurious transmission, it's generally fairly easy to pinpoint the location of the source. Let's say, however, that you're in a large, open space, such as a secretarial bullpen, where there are numerous cubicles divided by short wall partitions, and you spot a transmission whose source you wish to locate. Sweeping all the surfaces with a sniffer can be very tedious, and there's always the possibility you might miss the site by just enough to fail to get a noticeable reading on the

▲

sniffer. A device that can show the direction the signal is com-ing from would be ideal and would allow you to easily zero in on the transmitter.

Enter the RDF. Most of these units use an FM receiver that covers the bands of interest and some form of Doppler signal processor. The Doppler effect is what you notice when you hear, for example, a train go by. As the train approaches, the tone of its whistle is a constant pitch. As soon as it passes you and starts to recede, the pitch drops noticeably. When it's coming at you, the speed of the train is added to the speed of the sound wave, increasing its apparent frequency; as the train moves away, its speed is subtracted from the whistle's pitch and the tone appears to lower in frequency.

As employed in an RDF unit, the Doppler processor depends on a pair of antennas, usually short, vertical whips, separated by a few feet and mounted on a hand-held crossbar. This array is connected to the processor and then to an FM receiver, which is tuned to the frequency of the transmission in question. The processor switches its input rapidly back and forth between the two antennas. As you rotate the antenna array, one of the antennas will be closer to the transmission source than the other and there will be a phase difference between the two received signals. The output of the proces-sorñreceiver combination is connected to a readout device, usually a zero-center meter or LED display. When the line through the two antennas (i.e., the crossbar) is exactly perpen-dicular to the incoming wave, both antennas will be equidis-tant-distant from the source and the meter will read zero, or the middle of its range. Moving the array clockwise or counter-clockwise will bring one antenna closer to the source than the other, and the readout will deflect left or right to indi-cate this deviation. This allows you to point the array directly at the source of the transmission. Most units also contain a sig-nal-strength meter to give relative distance indications (see Appendix D).

This method is routinely used for tracking vehicles. A

▲

transmitter is secreted on the target vehicle and the RDF is mounted in the chase car, which allows the target vehicle to be tracked or located from several miles away. Vehicle-tracking RDF systems are covered in some depth in issues 23 and 24 of *Full Disclosure* [3] and there are several excellent books on radio direction finding available. [4] We also include in the appendices plans for an antenna array-processor unit that you can build and attach to your FM receiver to make a very functional, portable RDF system.

VIDEO TRANSMITTERS

A few final words here about video transmitters are in order. Over the past few years, equipment has become available permitting real-time transmission of video and audio from a small camera. Much of the developmental work in this area was done by amateur radio operators and assumed the acronym ATV for amateur television. This is a recent enough development that there are no clear-cut federal regulations in place (yet) and the legality issues involved in watching someone covertly are quite hazy. There is a proliferation of equipment and kits for small video transmission systems available for use by licensed hams and, needless to say, some of this technology has found its way into the surveillance field.

One factor to bear in mind is the bandwidth requirements. A typical video signal, with all its various timing, sync, and picture elements, takes up about 8 MHz of bandwidth. Because of the crowded nature and limited spectrum of the VHF ham bands, most ATV units operate on UHF bands at 430 MHz, 902 MHz, or 1.2 GHz. This also permits small antennas and compact transmitter design. Essentially, these are complete TV transmitting stations, identical to their higher-powered commercial counterparts.

From a covert surveillance operator's viewpoint, there are pros and cons to each band. The 430 MHz band is just below the lowest UHF TV channel, and because most TV receivers have manual tuning that extends slightly past the commercial band edge limits, a unit operating at, say, 438 MHz can usually be tuned directly in on a monitor TV. Unfortunately, anyone else within range hunting around at the low end of the dial can also see the picture.

The band from 902 to 928 MHz is probably the most popular. There's activity on the 1.2 GHz band as well, but the higher we go in frequency, the more we have the usual problems associated with microwaves (extremely limited bandwidth allocation, adverse atmospheric effects, line-of-sight requirement, and so on).

There's another reason the 902 MHz band is attractive. The FCC recently approved public use of the band under Part 15 of federal regulations, which covers devices intended for very-short-range transmissions. You can now purchase, over-the-counter and with no license, video transmitters designed to attach to your video cassette recorder, for example, that will transmit that signal to other rooms of the house, allowing you to watch tapes from the VCR on another TV located elsewhere without having to run interconnecting cables. These transmitters are limited by law to a certain maximum effective radiated power, which limits their useful range to about 120 feet. However, by modifying these units for battery operation, a useful short-range surveillance system results. One-hundred and twenty feet is often more than enough for covert monitoring, and the span of 902 to 928 MHz allows three 8-MHz-wide channels to transmit simultaneously.

Because this band is above the UHF TV channels, a converter between the receiving antenna and TV monitor is necessary. This takes the incoming signal—at 910 MI-Iz, for example—and converts it down to the 50-70 MHz region so that it may be tuned in with a standard TV on channel 2, 3, or 4. This has the added advantage of security; no one without a converter can accidentally tune across the transmission.

It is also fairly easy to add booster amps or gain blocks to the output of the transmitter to increase its range, which is ille-

▲

gal but quite commonplace. A converter unit should be a standard item in your tool kit, and both the 430 and 902 MHz bands should be checked if there is any suspicion of video monitoring.

INFRARED AND OPTICAL SYSTEMS

Before we finish this chapter, a few words about infrared and optical systems are in order. IR systems may be short-range, omnidirectional-directional affairs designed to transmit information through a window or doorway to a receiving/recording unit, or they may be optically focused arrays designed for ranges in the hundreds to thousands of feet. In both cases, standard RF sweep techniques are useless and special procedures need be employed.

Short-range arrays are typically a two-unit package that in many cases are modified versions of commercially available devices. A good example would be Radio Shack's wireless headset and transmitter (model 32-2050), which was originally intended to attach to your stereo and send the audio signal throughout the room on a modulated IR light beam. The headphones have an internally mounted IR receiver, and anywhere within the IR field they will intercept the light beam and convert it back to audio. The effective range is only 20 feet, but the devices are compact and may be adapted for battery operation. In practice, the microphone, a suitable mike preamplifier, and the IR transmitter are placed in the target site and the receiver/recorder combination is mounted on the opposite side of a common window or open doorway. One simple yet effective system we ran across had the microphone/transmitter combination mounted in a smoked-glass vase, which was placed on the table in a conference room. Any container that is optically transparent to infrared will work. The receiver/tape recorder was on the opposite side of a common window on a secretary's desk. This is a very discrete, easily deployed system that defeats detection by normal methods.

There are also focused systems that use lenses to con-

▲

centrate the transmitted signal into a narrow beam, which gives you vastly extended ranges. Several electronics hobby magazines have recently carried construction articles on focused IR systems.

There are several methods available to detect IR radiation. The simplest involves a small card that is sensitive to IR. These cards fluoresce or emit a visible light output when in the presence of IR signals. They must be in very close proximity to the source but they're cheap and effective. They're also a handy way of checking PIRs (passive IR) burglar alarm sensors for an output. Again, Radio Shack has a suitable model (276-099 for about $5.95). They will also detect some forms of laser transmissions.

One expensive yet effective method of IR detection involves night-vision goggles (NVGs), which are usually surplus items. These goggles make all forms of IR radiation visible, usually in shades of green. They are quite handy for evaluating alarm systems that employ PIRs as well.

It should be noted that video cameras or recorders equipped with infrared lenses (or other night vision equipment) will also detect IR radiation.

In the appendices we include plans for a small, battery-operated unit that picks up IR radiation from fair distances and gives a visual readout that indicates the direction of the incoming signal.

Laser systems are much more difficult to detect because you must be directly in the beam's path and have a receiver/detector tuned to the exact frequency of the transmitting laser. In Appendix C we list sources for laser transmitters and receivers.

The best protection against laser intrusion is the employment of preventative measures. Heavy drapes over any exterior windows will effectively defeat most systems. This falls under the area of client education, which should be a part of any sweep procedure. Thermopane or triple-glazed windows also minimize laser pick-up systems.

▲

• • •

In summary, to be a successful, professional countersurveillance technician, you need to know the frequencies and methods of transmission most likely to be employed by the other side. New technologies are emerging almost daily and it's important to keep up with progress in these fields.

There are certain tools and test devices that are imperative for a successful sweep and other items that, with the proper training and application, will greatly simplify your task. Even the most sophisticated equipment is useless, however, if you do not have a concise, organized method of employing them.

ENDNOTES

1. Printed circuit boards and parts kits for an inexpensive spectrum analyzer that can be added to any standard oscilloscope are available from Science Workshop, Box 310, Bethpage, New York 11714. A complete set of boards and parts, less cabinet and external controls, is in the $100 range. These are excellent kits that produce a finished product that will do almost everything its bigger brothers can do. Murray Barlowe, who runs Science Workshop, is also coming out with a book on spectrum analyzers soon that promises to be well worth reading.

2. Auto-Sweep, made by ECO-TEC, 1187 Waukechon St., Suite 9, Shawano, Wisc. 54166

3. Lieg, Peter. "Vehicle Tracking Systems: The Technical Side." *Full Disclosure* issues 23 and 24.

4. Moell, Joseph D. and Thomas N. Curlee. *Transmitter Hunting: Radio Direction Finding Simplified*. Blue Ridge Summit, PA: TAB Books, 1987. Aimed at the amateur radio operator, this is a very thorough treatment of radio direction finding that is quite useful for the countersurveillance technician.

Telephone Systems

By far, the most pervasive (some would say intrusive) piece of electronic technology is the telephone. There are more than 100 million telephones in the United States alone and any one of them may be interconnected with any other one by an unskilled operator simply by pressing the right sequence of numbered buttons.

Invented by Alexander Graham Bell in 1876, the rights to the invention have, until quite recently, been the property of AT&T. Whatever your feelings on monopolies, this arrangement allowed the construction of the support medium necessary to make the telephone system a viable means of communication. By itself, the telephone is quite useless, but attached to a far-flung network of cabling, reaching virtually every corner of the world, the phone system permits almost instantaneous communication between any two people on the face of the earth.

▲

It is this network of interconnecting wiring and the attendant switching stations that give the phone system its fantastic capabilities—and also its greatest potential for abuse. Any signal traveling down a pair of wires may be intercepted simply by tapping across those wires at any point between the two communicating parties.

To appreciate how easy this interception can be and to learn how to detect it when it is happening, a basic understanding of how the system functions is necessary.

When you lift the handset to place a call, the telephone alerts the switching exchange that a call is about to be made and lets you know the exchange is ready by emitting a dial tone. After you dial the number desired, the various interconnections are made and it indicates whether the call can be completed by either a ringing tone or a busy signal. It then rings a bell at the called party location to indicate the presence of an incoming call and makes the necessary connections. It breaks the connection when the handset is replaced on the telephone set.

While the call is in progress, the electronic signals representing your voice are sent down a pair of wires through various substations to a central exchange. They are then routed out through other substations to the called location. Signals between substations and the main exchange may be sent by microwave or even the relatively new method of fiber optics, which uses light pulses traveling down a "light pipe" or transparent fiber cable. In both cases, multiple calls can be transmitted simultaneously using multiplexing or time-sharing techniques. However, from the calling phone to the first substation, and from the last substation to the called party, only a single call exists on the wires at any given time. This is where taps can be made.

As we've pointed out before, "bugging" a phone refers to attaching a radio frequency transmitter to the phone lines, and sweeping is treated much the same as sweeping for a room-monitoring transmitter. "Tapping" a phone refers to intercepting the signal by means of a hard-wired connection from any point on the lines to a recording or monitoring location. We will be primarily concerned with phone taps in the following chapters, although most of the techniques used to indicate the presence of a tap on the lines will also show the insertion of a bugging transmitter within the system.

CELLULAR SYSTEMS

There has been a recent marriage between telephone technology and radio frequency electronics, first with the cordless phone and later with cellular phone networks. In both cases, some or all of the hard-wired network is replaced with a radio frequency transmitter link. Upcoming developments in direct-to-satellite calls are extensions of this technology.

In the case of cellular or portable phones, the signal from the calling phone is transmitted on a radio wave at approximately 800 MHz and is picked up by a nearby repeater transceiver. Tower-mounted and spaced at intervals over large areas of the country, these repeaters pick up the 800 MHz signal and translate it to a higher frequency somewhere in the microwave range. It is then beamed in a line-of-sight transmission to the next repeater and so on, leap-frogging through the network until it reaches the repeater nearest the called party, where it is sent out in the original 800 MHz band for reception by the called phone.

At either end of this link, the signal exists in the air as a normal voice RF transmission, and both sides of the conversation may be intercepted by anyone with a radio receiver tuned to the correct frequency.

Listening to these conversations covertly is illegal, but there is virtually no way this practice can be detected short of catching the perpetrator in the act. Law enforcement agencies routinely monitor these frequencies as well. There is a story circulating about a dealer who set up a major drug buy using

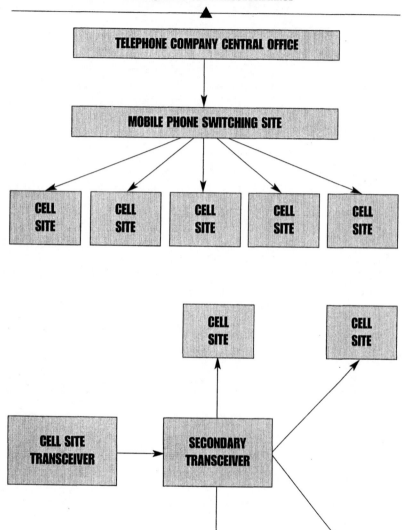

The telephone company's basic system.

▲

his cellular phone, hung up, and then placed a call ordering a pizza and giving his home address. The DEA showed up before the pizza did. Needless to say, this is a very insecure line of communication and your clients should be so informed if they aren't alert to the fact already. Absolutely no confidential information should be discussed on cordless or cellular phones as there is virtually no way of knowing who might be eavesdropping on the transmissions.

FAX AND COMPUTER LINKS

There are two other relatively recent blends of telephone and electronic disciplines that should be of concern to the countersurveillance technician. The first of these involves computers and modems (modulator/demodulator). A modem takes input and output information from a computer at location A and converts it to tones that can be transmitted via the phone lines to a computer at location B. This permits two computers to interlink and exchange information, or permits a smaller computer to tie into the memory bank and data-processing circuitry of a larger, central mainframe computer. Obviously, much information sent in this fashion is confidential in nature, but coding schemes are rarely used, so unauthorized interception by a third party is a distinct possibility.

Another even more prevalent use of the phone lines involves sending copies of documents with a fax machine. Similar to having a Xerox machine hooked up to both ends of a phone connection, the data again is sent as a series of tones, which are converted back into characters at the receiving end and printed onto paper. Again, at any point on the transmission path, another fax machine may be inserted surreptitiously and the entire transmission may be copied.

The important factor here is that no additional connections need be made to the computer or the fax machine. If there is a tap in place on the phone line, whatever information is present on the line is compromised.

▲

One advantage for the surveillance operator when tapping or bugging phone systems is the presence of a voltage across the lines whether the phone is in use or not. This eliminates the need for batteries or a connection to an AC source for power. There are typically four wires entering a site for telephone connection: red, green, yellow, and black. Only the red (the "ring" connection) and green (the "tip" connection) usually need to be attached for proper operation of the system. (The terms derive from the one-quarter-inch phone plugs used to make connections in old-time, manual exchange switchboards. In some older phone systems, the yellow wire must be tied to the green, which is normally done internally.)

When the phone is on-hook, 48 volts exist across the red and green wires. This drops to about five volts when off-hook. Even five volts are more than enough to power a transmitter bug or a line-transmitting unit. In addition, because this voltage is supplied by the phone company on its own wires, it is in no way dependent on local 110-volt AC power. Even in the event of a power blackout due to storm or emergency, the phone system usually continues to function. The phone company also thoughtfully provides lightning protectors at the cable entrance, which will also protect surveillance gear placed down-line from them.

BUGS

First, let's deal with RF transmitting bugs. As we've previously discussed, these can usually be located by standard RF sweep techniques. The problem is that many of these transmitters are dormant (inoperative) unless the phone is off-hook and a call is in progress. This can be overcome by placing a call on the phone in question. Dial your office answering machine, the time-and-temperature report, or any other number you know will be answered so that a completed connection may be established, and then sweep for RF transmissions in the usual fashion.

However, most of the procedures employed to locate a

▲

hard-wired tap will also reveal the presence of an RF bug, dormant or not. Connection methods fall into four categories: "leech" transmitters (both series and parallel, plus a battery-operated unit connected in parallel) and induction pick-ups, which typically require no operating power.

Leech transmitters are those that obtain their operating power from the voltage present on the phone lines, typically five volts in the off-hook mode. A series-connected unit is spliced in-line with one of the wires, usually the red. A parallel-connected leech unit is bridged across both wires. If proper impedance (AC resistance) levels are observed, both of these are difficult to detect.

There is, however, a limited amount of power that can be leeched from the phone lines before the apparent impedance changes noticeably or the five volts starts to drop or rise. In reality, these amount to the same thing. If an extended transmitting range is required, a battery power supply must be used to prevent unacceptable loading on the phone's power system. These battery-operated units are usually wired in a parallel configuration.

Induction pick-ups overcome these problems because they have no direct connection to any of the phone wiring and therefore present no loading whatsoever. They are also quick and easy to install. Functionally, the pick-up is a small, multi-turn coil of wire, often equipped with a suction cup for easy external attachment (although covert surveillance usually dictates placing the pick-up inside the phone handset or housing), which is installed close enough to the large inductors (coils) present inside the phone to intercept part of the magnetic field produced by these inductors. This field induces a voltage in the pick-up coil that is an exact duplicate of the signals on the phone lines. From there it goes to a transmitter input (in the case of a bug) or is hard-wired to a recording or monitoring station (in the case of a tap). These hook-ups usually include a 60 Hz notch filter to remove any hum pickup from adjacent power wiring.

▲

BUG ZAPPING

There are several methods used to locate or disable bugs and taps. Besides RE sweeping for bugs and physical inspections, both of which we've covered, some technicians use the shotgun approach. This involves sending a very-high-voltage—usually several thousand volts—pulse down the phone lines, which effectively zaps any bugs or recording devices connected to the lines. Of course, the phone must be disconnected first, and the lines must also be disconnected from the incoming service feed to prevent destroying equipment at the substation or exchange. Induction pickups are occasionally immune to these tactics and spike protectors can be built into the bugs or recorders to damp out these high-voltage spikes. They work most of the time.

VOLTAGE—IMPEDANCE MEASUREMENTS

Besides the approaches mentioned above, there are two broad categories of test techniques used to indicate anomalies on the phone lines. The first one involves devices that measure the impedance and off-hook voltage of the lines, looking for deviations from normal. The problem is, a properly designed and installed bug can be almost invisible to these methods.

TIME DOMAIN REFLECTOMETRY

Time domain reflectometry (TDR) is a sophisticated (and expensive) method of analyzing the physical condition of phone lines. Under the proper set of preconditions, its use can indicate changes from the last reading with great accuracy. It can also indicate the distance from the measurement point at which the discontinuity exists. In the next chapter, we'll cover all these approaches and discuss currently available diagnostic equipment.

▲

• • •

If the phones at your target site are being monitored by law enforcement groups or a federal agency, chances are you'll never know. But even they have to get a court order under Title 3 (see Appendix A) if they wish to use the evidence in court. They generally have the cooperation of the phone companies and the tapping can be done way down the line at one of the exchanges, where it will never show up on your tests.

The best advice to your clients is to send absolutely nothing of a sensitive nature over a phone that you have any reason whatsoever to suspect is compromised.

Telephone Line Analysis

As is the case with RF sweeping, phone line analysis is most successful when a standardized, routine procedure is followed. The first step is the physical inspection, which is usually much more straightforward than an inspection for room monitoring transmitters because any taps or bugs must be attached to the phone or its incoming wires. Disassemble and inspect the telephone set first, looking for any foreign objects or connections inside. Repetition breeds familiarity and you should soon be able to instantly recognize anything unusual.

PHYSICAL CHECKS

The next step involves following the wires backwards from the phone as far as possible, hopefully all the way to the service entrance to the premises. This is the point where the wires from the telephone pole enter. In many cases, from this

▲

point upstream (toward the central exchange) the wires are either high off the ground, as in an aerial feed, or buried underground. If there is a pedestal termination block (these are often green fiberglass boxes several inches square and several feet high where all the individual feeds for a given area converge for connection to a multiple conductor feed from the phone company) inspect the lock for damage or tampering (taps or bugs can easily be installed here). From this point upstream, it is unlikely there would be any compromised wiring.

If you can physically trace each line back to this point without finding any covert connections, you can be reasonably certain the line is clean. All extension phone lines should be traced back to their common interconnect points and multi-line phones should have each line checked individually.

VOLTAGE AND IMPEDANCE CHECKS

In many cases it is difficult, if not impossible, to check every inch of every line, especially in business offices with many lines and extensions or in buildings with wiring enclosed in walls. Even if you think the lines are physically clean, a voltage and impedance check should be performed.

Most of the commonly available bug-and-tap detectors are designed to indicate anomalies in these two parameters. As we've said, the normal voltage between the red and green wires on a phone feed should be about 48 volts when all phones are on-hook, and drop to five volts or so when they are off-hook. If there is, for example, a series connection for a bug and you measure the voltage upstream of the connection, there will be a five-volt drop across the phone and another drop across the bug. The apparent voltage measured upstream will be the sum of these drops, which is usually only slightly higher than five volts.

If there is a parallel connection for a bug or a tap, additional current will flow through the tap and the apparent voltage will be less than five volts. These measurements must be

▲

carried out with the phone lines connected because they supply the operating voltage. The best procedure is to first make sure the phone is clean; substitute one of your own that you know is OK if in doubt. Take a reading at the phone with the receiver off-hook and then repeat the reading as far upstream as you can get; the readings should be the same and both should be very close to five volts. In Appendix B we've explained how to take a simple device with a modular plug input and output that can easily be inserted at these points to take a reading. It's basically a Y connector with a built-in voltmeter connected across the line. In both cases, the on-hook voltages should also be identical (close to 48 volts).

At this point, one disconnects either or both leads (red and green) at the service entrance and measures the resistance at both the phone end and service entrance end of the line(s). A normal resistance reading is more difficult to specify because of differences in phone designs, but the readings should be essentially equal. The reading at the service entrance end may be slightly higher due to the resistance of the additional wiring, but this should be on the order of a couple of ohms or less. Anything higher indicates a series tap and anything lower than the phone-end reading indicates a parallel connection.

Most designers try to keep the resistance of a series-inserted bug as low as possible to prevent appreciable voltage drop across it, whereas the goal for a parallel connection is extremely high resistance (to prevent loading down the line and pulling down the voltage). If properly designed, they are difficult to detect with either measurement method. The readings should be taken, however, because a surprisingly high percentage of bugs and taps are not properly designed.

TIME DOMAIN REFLECTOMETRY CHECKS

The only truly foolproof method of detecting a connection somewhere on the line (series or parallel) involves the use

▲

of TDR techniques. In simple terms, a TDR unit sends a pulsed signal down the cable and looks for reflected signals bouncing back up the line. At any point where there is a discontinuity in the normal impedance of the cable, a portion of the pulsed signal will be reflected back toward the source. By measuring the time it takes for this return pulse to appear and by knowing the propagation speed of the signal down and back up different types of cabling, a distance reading can be computed to tell the operator how far down the wire the discontinuity exists. Used extensively by cable TV companies to locate breaks and bad stretches of coax, the system is effective for distances of many thousands of feet and is extremely accurate and sensitive.

Unfortunately, it is also extremely expensive, test gear being in the several thousand dollar range. If you plan on doing a considerable amount of phone system analysis, however, this device will pay for itself in short order.

The one major limitation with this procedure is the necessity for a measurement of the same system that is under test when it is in a known "clean" condition. This is called a "signature signal" and is used for comparison against the signal received when the line is being tested for compromised conditions. It is vital to know the line is clean when doing the signature analysis; if a bug or tap is present at this point, the signature will be contaminated and future readings are meaningless. Anyone telling you the system will detect bugs without first having a signature of the same system when it is known to be clean is outright lying.

Because of this, this method is most useful for repeat analyses of systems, such as you would have in a service contract situation, where you might routinely and periodically check the same lines on a continuing basis. Any change from the original clean signature would indicate something had changed radically since the last check.

▲

VOX RECORDERS AND PEN REGISTERS

There are a couple of devices that are normally hard-wired (tapped) into phone lines at the site. The first category involves voice-operated audio tape recorders (VOX tape recorders). Telecorder and others manufacture recorders that attach to a modular jack present well-balanced, virtually undetectable loads to the line; and record all outgoing and incoming calls automatically. A suitable line interface circuit and a standard VOX tape recorder will accomplish the same thing. Normally, only a physical inspection will reveal their location.

Pen registers are connected in similar fashion and present the same detection difficulties. These devices record the dialed number, date and time of all out-going calls. A combination unit [1] records number, date and time of outgoing calls; and date, time, and both sides of the conversation for both outgoing and incoming calls. Again, a physical inspection is the best detection method.

• • •

Remember that a physical inspection is the best method for finding taps and bugs on phone lines. The phones themselves, every inch of accessible cabling, and the service entrance should all be inspected. Voltage and impedance checks will reveal careless installations and poorly designed taps and bugs, but a TDR test with a suitable signature signal for reference is the best technique.

Above all, customer education as to the insecure nature of telephone communication is the ultimate preventative measure. Current customers should be told that if they suspect phone line tampering and wish to contact you for a sweep, to use a pay phone or other unit known to be clean.

▲

ENDNOTES

1. Available from Eco-Tec, 1187 Waukechon St., Suite 9, Shawano, WI 54166

Intrusion Alarm Electronic Countermeasures

In this chapter we'll outline two additional services you may wish to offer your client. While neither is necessary for completion of a successful sweep, both will prevent headaches for you and your client.

Evaluation of intrusion alarms is rarely done. In many cases the client had such systems installed merely to get a cut in his insurance premiums. Unfortunately, as an industry, the alarm installation business is no better than the countersurveillance business in terms of ignorance and incompetence.

PIRs, field sensors, sound-activated systems, photoelectric eyes, hard-wired perimeter networks, sirens, and automatic phone dialers are intermixed in many system designs with little thought as to their ultimate effectiveness. Many of the people who understand these systems best are not installing them, but rather defeating them for criminal purposes.

A complete vetting of a premises should include a

▲

comprehensive evaluation of all alarm systems. Because a good countersurveillance technician must learn to think like an operative from the other side, who better than you to do this evaluation?

An intrusion alarm usually consists of a central control panel, power supply, entrance deactivation system, and warning device. This assembly is connected to a series of sensors that detect movement or tampering. The central control panel monitors the status of all sensors and triggers the warning device whenever a sensor is activated. The warning device may be a siren or an automatic telephone dialer, which alerts the owner, the authorities, or a central monitoring service. Some systems employ closed-circuit TV (CCTV) cameras connected to a monitoring station or to a VCR tape machine. Smoke detectors may be included to alert one to the possibility of fire at the site. The central control supplies power for the sensors and usually has a back-up battery supply to permit operation in the event AC power is interrupted and has a defeat mode to allow entrance by authorized parties. This defeat mode may be accessed via a key switch at an outside entrance, a keypad similar to an electronic combination lock, a card-access ("cardex") system, or a delay circuit, the latter of which allows a certain time period to pass before activation of the warning device, thus permitting the owner to enter and deactivate the system.

The two most common forms of pick-up are field (motion) sensors and perimeter devices, such as magnetic door switches and window breakage sensors. Field sensors are usually PIR devices, which are circuits that flood an area with an IR light field—which is invisible to the naked eye, you'll recall—and look for reflected signals or disturbances of the field caused by an object or person in motion within the field. Some will also respond to body heat. Sound-activated sensors are also occasionally employed.

Perimeter devices are usually door switches (which may be mechanical or magnetic), conductive tape patterns on windows, breakage or vibration pickups for windows, pressure and mat switches triggered by someone walking on them, and photoelectric beams to protect a long expanse of wall surface or entrance areas. These sensors may be wired in a series configuration, which uses normally closed pickups so that any one of them opening will cause current in the series loop to be interrupted, thereby triggering the control unit and warning device(s). They may also be wired in parallel, usually dictating normally open sensors; any closure trips the main control.

Series-connected circuits, although occasionally more difficult to wire, provide the added protection of total loop security. This means anyone cutting the interconnecting wire at any point sets off the alarm. To deactivate a sensor on a door, let's say, it would be necessary to first install a bypass wire across the sensor and then clip the sensor lead inside the shunt. Parallel-connected sensors can usually be clipped off without effect, but they typically cannot be shunted. Field sensors are much more difficult to bypass, but are usually restricted to coverage of interior areas.

The best approach is to start with a floor plan of the area being analyzed. Mark all protected entrances and windows on the blueprint. Each door and window sensor should be checked for proper operation. Using an IR monitoring device, check the operation and area of coverage of all PIRs and field sensors and shade in these areas on the floor plan. PIRs can also be checked by slowly moving about in the general area and noting how far away the device can detect motion.

After you have all covered areas marked or shaded in on the floor plan, vulnerable areas will be obvious. Don't overlook possible entrance points such as skylights, garage doors, large ventilation ducts, flimsy Sheetrock partitions between your area and an unprotected adjacent one, and open spaces above drop ceilings common to other unprotected rooms.

If you note glaring omissions in the coverage pattern, additional sensors can be added. If the added sensors are needed in an area quite remote from the control panel, RF

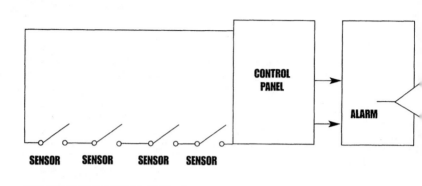

The series alarm system.

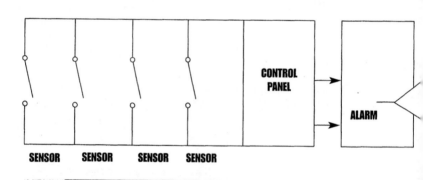

The parallel alarm system.

transmitter-linked devices may be employed to eliminate having to run connecting cables on finished walls. There usually is no such thing as too many sensors. However, be aware of overly sensitive situations. Dogs, cats, and other large pets can trigger field alarms, as can drapes or curtains moving in the breeze from heating and air-conditioning systems. Vibration sensors and sound-activated systems can be triggered by hail, heavy wind, or someone pounding on the door after hours.

▲

Too many false alarms from a system generate a cry-wolf syndrome, which is as bad as having no system at all. It also ticks off the cops after several dry runs. Many cities charge for responding to a false alarm and everyone's confidence in the system falters.

WARNING DEVICES

The warning device is usually a siren and or an automatic phone dialer with a taped message.

Sirens

Sirens are usually mounted in an inaccessible spot to prevent tampering or disabling and are generally battery-operated because of heavy current demands when activated. (Check the battery!) They are most effective for discouraging petty thievery or vandalism by amateurs; a pro realizes he has a limited amount of time before anyone can respond and makes the most of this delay.

Phone Dialers

Phone dialers interface directly to the phone lines and can place up to three consecutive calls to prerecorded numbers (they play a taped message; check for proper operation.) They have no way of repeating the call if the line is busy. Many police departments have a dedicated line for automated dialers to minimize the likelihood of a busy signal. It's usually necessary to fill out some forms for the police listing principals in the business who should be contacted in case of an emergency. One further note: dialers are illegal on party lines because the possibility of a malfunction tying up the entire party line.

Some states disallow dialers that contact law enforcement agencies directly. The theory is that when police monitor a private alarm company's installation, they are getting into the private sector, which is generally prohibited. Actually, this

▲

scam is perpetrated by the alarm companies themselves, usually in conjunction with some private monitoring service. Your alarm is tripped, the dialer notifies the monitoring service, and the service contacts the police. This added link in the chain just allows more time for the burglar to burgle before the police show up. Some monitoring services may not even be in the same state as the system they're watching. It does keep the monitoring service in business, however, and this can be a very lucrative situation. Some alarm companies sell their systems at ridiculously low prices (one even gives them away free) if the customer signs a multi-year monitoring contract. This is a captive audience situation and should be avoided at all costs. The best approach is to have the dialer notify three principals in the business at their home numbers (call forwarding can be used) and have them call the police.

Phone dialers can be used without a siren for a silent alarm system, thus increasing the possibility of catching the intruder in the act. One important item to check is the security of all exposed phone wiring exterior to the site as well as the junction box and any exposed terminal blocks. Put the lines in conduit if they are vulnerable, and secure all boxes. (PVC conduit is preferable if local code allows it because it can't be disassembled with just a screwdriver.) If a burglar suspects a dialer system is installed, all he has to do is cut the phone lines outside the building and the site is left totally unprotected.

CCTV Systems

Many business use CCTV systems, which are run to a monitoring station (a building security guard, for instance), a time-lapse VCR (which will record on a brief, repeatable basis all night long), or a triggered VCR system (which only records when there is activity at the site.) One system uses a VCR triggered from an RF transmitter attached to the sensors, which permits rapid set up and allows easy changing the location of the sensors.[1]

There are also systems that allow you to dial a phone at the site that is connected to a camera. Similar to the video-phone, the system sends slow-scan pictures (approximately one frame every 15 seconds) to the caller's location so he can monitor activity at the site from anywhere else. Pan, tilt, and zoom modes of the camera can also be remotely controlled.

Small, portable video transmitters, such as those covered in Chapter 4, can also be used to send sound and picture to a VCR via radio waves, which permits rapid deployment and easy relocation. They may be triggered on by motion sensors to conserve battery life, and there are circuits for the VCR to keep it in standby until there is an active transmission. These systems are used extensively to prevent shoplifting and employee theft.

The general approach is to analyze the coverage of the system, looking for weak spots (this is also an opportunity to sell additional needed equipment to the client if you have access to appropriate product lines). The next step involves checking every component of the system for proper operation. This is an excellent option to offer on a service contract and can increase the profitability of a job significantly. Besides, if you don't find a bug during the sweep portion of the job, you can inform the client that it would be difficult for anyone to gain access to plant one later if his intrusion alarm is in good working order.

Private Investigators

There is one other possibility that should be explored. A few states (Arizona, for example) require the presence of a licensed private detective at all sweeps. This is a totally ridiculous requirement and is being challenged in court. Nonetheless, a good working relationship with a licensed private investigation firm is helpful (they can usually put you on as an apprentice). Private investigators are a close-knit group and you might be surprised at how many referrals they can generate. If you follow this route, you can offer employee vetting as a service to your clients. Background checks on new employees or those under suspicion can be easily handled by any competent private investigative agency, and many of these firms would love to have a good countersurveillance technician at their disposal.

ELECTRONIC COUNTERMEASURES

One area that's becoming increasingly important in the field of countersurveillance is electronic countermeasures (ECM). Unless a client is rich enough or paranoid enough to hire a full-time on-staff countersurveillance expert, he may still have problems on any given day. Even ongoing service contracts with a reputable countersurveillance firm do not prevent the possibility of infestation between visits.

All of the areas we've discussed can be covered by ECM procedures. In many cases, these techniques overlap. A good security system can prevent hard-wired systems, bugs, and phone taps from being deployed. In-house security and visitor screening should be standard practice. Above all, a competent analysis of all areas of vulnerability should be done by professionals.

Contact and spike mikes can usually be masked by attaching an ultrasonic vibration generator to the walls. Generating this same sound through an appropriate speaker will also flood the interior of the room with the same masking ability as the ultrasonic vibration generator. Above the range of audibility for humans, it'll drive your dog crazy.

ECM for RF bugs can take two forms: detection and masking. Company personnel can be supplied with and trained in the use of RF sniffers. As discussed in Chapter 4, automated sweep techniques can be employed.

Masking of RF bug transmissions can take a couple of forms. One may attempt to cover up the bug's signal with locally generated, wide-band short-range RF noise. Units are available that work like an RF sniffer in reverse—they put out

▲

a field of random signals on all frequencies most likely to be employed for covert transmissions. Obviously, the range needs to be carefully plotted (you don't want to wipe out the neighbor's FM reception, which guarantees a visit from the FCC). Similar techniques exist for IR systems (the room may be hooded with steady-state IR from a simple generator, effectively covering any modulated beams from a bug).

Another technique involves creating a containment zone, thereby keeping any transmissions bottled up. RF design engineers use what is called a "screen room" when designing RF circuits. Also known as a Farady shield, this is a room totally enclosed with a fine-mesh, grounded metal screen. This keeps any outside signals from entering and affecting the circuit under design. We want to apply the principle in reverse. The same type of room can keep any signals from leaving. A screened conference room is typical in that even if someone carries a transmitter into a meeting on his person, the signal will be stopped at the screened walls. This is standard practice at embassies—all sensitive discussions take place inside a shielded room.

Hidden video cameras present more of a problem. If connected to a transmitter, the above RF techniques should suffice, but hard-wired systems or video briefcases are more difficult. Short of holding meetings in the dark, not much can be done. IR flooding will disable some cameras sensitive to this range, but many employ IR filters internal to the lens.

There are several devices on the market designed for permanent connection to a telephone. They basically read the same parameters we covered in the section on phone line analysis, indicating over-or-under values of voltage and impedance continuously. They are no more or no less accurate than manual checks, but should indicate the presence of a great majority of bugs and taps.

Keep in mind that the best form of ECM is common sense and diligence. A healthy degree of paranoia in your clients is well advised.

▲

ENDNOTES

1. The Institute of Private Investigative Studies, 8129 N. 35th Ave, #134, Phx, AZ 85051. All kinds of books, videos, and magazines on investigations.

Specifying, Pricing, and Service Contracts

Probably more difficult than the actual sweep is the problem of quoting and billing a job. On one hand, you have a trained staff on payroll and a healthy investment in test gear. On the other hand, the industry is relatively new, beset by incompetence, and beyond the understanding of the prospective client. If you were hired to repair a roof or tune a car, your customer at least has a rudimentary understanding of the problems involved. When you sell a sweep, the client generally has no idea of what constitutes a professional approach.

Unfortunately, there are usually no guidelines or license requirements needed to advertise yourself as a countersurveillance technician. All you need is a business card and enough test gear, replete with all the bells and whistles, to snow the customer.

This is reminiscent of the early days of satellite dish installations—the field is wide open to promoters and hustlers

▲

and the average client has no idea of what he's buying. There are numerous firms that promise to solve every possible problem and arrive with a ton of test gear and a technical rap that would shame a junk-bond salesman. Winston Arrington 1 refers to this process as a "rain dance," and we used to call it a dog-and-pony show. In either case, fly-by-night outfits permeate the business, and you, as a professional, must be extra careful not to get dragged down by their mistakes.

The best approach is a preliminary meeting with a prospective client at which a bid for specific services is presented, followed by a signed contract if accepted. A calm, confident, caring approach works best; don't badger the client into services he doesn't want or need but educate him as best you can to the utility of various approaches. Whenever possible, push the concept of a service contract. If the customer is paranoid today about compromised communications, he'll likely be so tomorrow as well. A few repeat customers such as this can pay the rent and help defray the cost of that new analyzer you're drooling over. Don't be afraid to ask for a retainer; if a customer with a retainer calls in a panic, he'll expect immediate service and a quick response is worth whatever you can charge.

Some operatives charge for sweep services based on the total square footage of the site. However, because of the widely varying complexity of a sweep for an office versus a sweep of a warehouse, for example, we prefer to charge by the hour. Typical hourly rates are $50 for the senior technician/team leader, $40 for assistant technicians, and $20 for gophers. In most cases, an estimate of total time is presented up front, usually in the form of a "cost not to exceed" basis. Don't be afraid to charge for your time. If you do the job right, your bill will pale in comparison to the potential damage if the client's site is compromised.

The thing to remember is that you're on the defensive. The surveillance operative always has an advantage—he hides it and you have to find it. This automatically dictates a

▲

success rate of less than 100 percent. With all the technological choices he has, it is virtually impossible to find every bug he plants, which may be remotely activated, planted far enough up the line to prevent testing access, or be so cleverly concealed as to defeat the most comprehensive search. You can only do the best job possible within technical and time constraints. Your contract should reflect this situation. Remember, what you're selling is peace of mind. If you can reasonably assure your client of a disinfected premises, both of you should feel satisfied.

No matter how you phrase your contracts, keep a good lawyer on retainer. Have him check all your paperwork and keep alert for possible snags in the relationship with your client. If it is a commercial account and you're in doubt about the character of the customer, call the Better Business Bureau and see if he's been sued often or has a penchant for instigating legal actions from his end. Above all, don't be afraid to list any areas you feel may require ongoing analysis to prevent a compromised situation.

Title 3

WIRETAPPING AND
ELECTRONIC SURVEILLANCE

From Public Law 90-351

June 19, 1968

2512. Manufacture, distribution, possession and advertising of wire or oral communication intercepting devices prohibited.

(1) Except as otherwise specifically provided in this chapter, any person who willfully-

(a) sends through the mail, or sends or carries in interstate or foreign commerce, any electronic, mechanical, or other

▲

device, knowing or having reason to know that the design of such device renders it primarily useful for the purpose of the surreptitious interception of wire or oral communications;

(b) manufactures, assembles, or possesses, or sells any electronic, mechanical, or other device, knowing or having reason to know that the design of such device renders it primarily useful for the purpose of the surreptitious interception of wire or oral communications, and that such device or any component thereof has been or will be sent through the mail or transported in interstate or foreign commerce; or

(c) places in any newspaper, magazine, handbill or other publication any advertisement of

(i) any electronic, mechanical, or other device knowing or having reason to know that the design of such device renders it primarily useful for the purpose of surreptitious interception of wire or oral communication; or

(ii) any other electronic, mechanical, or other device, where such advertisement promotes the use of such device for the purpose of the surreptitious interception of wire or oral communications, knowing or having reason to know that such advertisement will be sent through the mail or transported in interstate or foreign commerce, shall be fined not more than $10,000 or imprisoned not more than five years or both.

(2) It shall not be unlawful under this section for-

(b) an officer, agent, or employee of, or a person under contract with, the United States, a State, or a political subdivision thereof, in the normal course of the activities of the United States, a State, or a political subdivision thereof, to send through the mail, send or carry in interstate or foreign commerce, or manufacture, assemble, possess, or sell, any electronic, mechanical, or other device knowing or having reason to know that the design of such device renders it primarily useful for the purpose of the surreptitious interception of wire or oral communications.

Construction Plans and Diagrams

RADIO FREQUENCY SNIFFER

This circuit for a countersurveillance monitor or RF sniffer was developed by Vincent Vollono and appeared in the November 1991 issue of *Popular Electronics*. It is reprinted here with their permission.

This is essentially a highly sensitive, wide-band receiver. When it detects a signal ranging from 1 to 2,000 MHz, it generates an audio output that ranges from a low growl (for a weak signal) to a high-pitched squeal (as the signal strength increases). In other words, the closer you get, the higher the pitch of the audio output. This allows you to sweep an area with the sniffer to determine the location of the transmitting device.

An important feature of the bug detector is its RF gain stage, which is centered around a high-gain microwave tran-

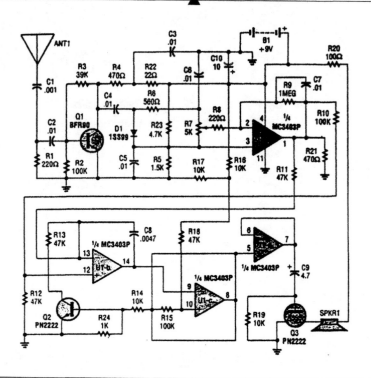

The countersurveillance monitor is built around UI (an MC3403P quad op-amp), three transistors (Q1-Q3), and a few support components.

sistor, thus greatly improving sensitivity. By increasing the antenna and setting the sensitivity control to its maximum level, extremely weak signals may be easily located. On the other hand, by decreasing antenna length and lowering the sensitivity setting, strong signals can be tracked down. Powered from a nine-volt transistor radio battery, the circuit draws very little current, making for long battery life.

The figure above shows a schematic diagram of the countersurveillance monitor. The circuit, built around a single integrated circuit (U1, an MC3403P quad op-amp), three transistors (Q1-Q3), and a few support components, receives its input from the antenna. That signal is fed through a high-pass

▲

PARTS LIST FOR THE COUNTERSURVEILLANCE MONITOR

SEMICONDUCTORS
UI—MC3403P quad op-amp. integrated circuit
QI—BFR9O or MFR9O1 NPN microwave transistor
Q2, Q3—PN2222 general-purpose NPN silicon transistor
D1—1SS99,ECG-112, or equivalent silicon diode

RESISTORS
(All fixed resistors are /4-watt, 5% units.)
R1, R8—220-ohm
R2, R10, R15—100,000-ohm
R3—39, 000-ohm
R4, R21—470-ohm
R5—1500-ohm
R6—560-ohm
R7—5000-ohm potentiometer
R9—1-megohm
R11—R13, R18—47,000-ohm
R14, R16, R17, R19—10,000-ohm
R20—1OO-ohm
R22—22-ohm
R23—4700-ohm
R24—1OOO-ohm

CAPACITORS
Cl—.OOl-uF, ceramic-disc
C2—C7—.Ol-uF, ceramic-disc
CS— 0047-uF, ceramic-disc
C9—4.7-uF, 16-WVDC, radial-lead electrolytic
ClO—lO-uF, 16-WVDC, axial-lead electrolytic

ADDITIONAL PARTS AND MATERIALS
SI—SPST toggle switch
B 1—9-volt transistor-radio battery
ANTI—Telescoping antenna
SPKR 1—8-ohm. 02-watt, 2 1/4-inch, speaker
Perfboard materials, enclosure, battery connector, battery holder (optional),
IC socket (optional). wire, solder, hardware, etc.

filter formed by C1, C2, and Ri, which eliminates bothersome 60 Hz pickup from any nearby power lines or line cords located in and around buildings and homes.

From the high-pass filter the signal is applied to transistor Q1, which provides a 10-dB gain for frequencies in the 1- to 2,000-MHz range for amplification. Resistors R2, R3, and R4 form the biasing network for Q1. The amplified signal is then AC coupled, via capacitor C4 and resistor R7's wiper (the sensitivity control) to the inverting input (pin 2) of U1-a. Op-amp U1 is configured as a very high-gain amplifier. With no signal input from the antenna, the output of U1-a at pin 1 is near ground potential.

When a signal from the antenna is applied to the base of Q1, it turns on, producing a negative-going voltage at the cathode of D1. That voltage is applied to pin 2 of U1-a, which amplifies and inverts the signal, producing a positive-going output at pin 1. Op-amps U1-b and U1-c along with C8, R1O-R18 and Q2 are arranged to form a

This full-size template for the countersurveillance monitor printed circuit artwork is provided for those who wish to etch their own boards. For those not so inclined, a pre-etched and predrilled board, as well as the parts that mount on or connect to it, can be purchased from the supplier listed in the parts list.

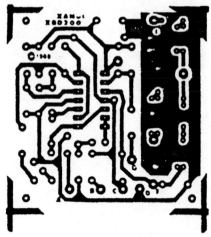

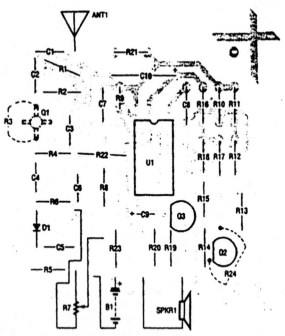

Assemble the printed circuit board using this parts-replacement diagram as a guide. Note that transistor Q1 and resistors R3 and R24 (all of which are shown as dashed lines) must be installed on the copper side of the board.

▲

voltage-controlled oscillator (VCO) that operates over the audio frequency range. As the output of U1-a increases, the frequency of the VCO increases. The VCO output at pin 8 of U1-c is fed to the input of U1-d, which is configured as a non-inverting, unity-gain (buffer) amplifier. The output of U1-d is used to drive Q3, which in turn drives the speaker.

Construction

The countersurveillance monitor was assembled on a preetched, predrilled printed circuit board. There is also a full-size template of the printed circuit artwork for those who wish to etch their own board.

Note that transistor Q1, as well as resistors R3 and R24 (which are shown as dashed lines on figure 3), must be installed on the copper side of the board. Because Q1 is a microwave transistor, special care must be taken when installing it and its leads should be kept as short as possible.

After completion and inspection for solder bridges and such, attach a nine-volt battery and rotate R7. You should get a siren-like sound, which should increase or decrease in pitch as R7 is rotated. Turning R7 fully counter-clockwise should stop the sound.

When using the unit to detect a bug, set the sensitivity low enough to avoid signals from nearby radio and TV stations. It may take some experimenting at first, but it should quickly become quite easy. Testing may be done with a walkie-talkie or a cordless phone to simulate a surveillance transmitter. When you get within a foot or two of an actual bug, there is no mistaking it for another signal—the audio pitch will be driven to its highest frequency.

If you have trouble locating Q1, try Radio Shack; they have an MFR901 available under the listing of "microwave transistor."

RADIO DIRECTION FINDER

The following construction article by Paul Bohrer,

W9DUU, appeared in the July 1990 issue of *73 Amateur Radio* (P.O. Box 60, Hancock, NH 03449) and is reprinted with their permission.

How often have you wished for a simple RDF which would work on just about any band and provide you with both an aural and visual means of determining the direction of a signal? The circuit described below processes information from two quarter or half wave antennas and gives right or left indications of which way to turn the antenna array so you can aim at the source. This type of RDF is called "homing" because it tells you which way to go to home in on the signal. It is not affected by signal strength, and as such will allow you to take readings on the move. This helps you to average out multi-path problems. You might bear in mind, however, that signal strength readings are still valuable, as they help confirm when you are almost on top of the transmitter.

How The Circuit Works

IC-1 produces a square-wave signal which is used to switch between the two antennas at an audio rate. The square wave from IC-1 also feeds through Q1, 2 and 3 with the result that there are square-wave signals of opposite polarity applied to each side of the 0-center meter.

When no audio from the receiver is present, the 5k zero pot is adjusted so that equal amplitudes of opposite polarity square-wave signal are developed across the 100 uF cap and the meter, with respect to the 4 volts reference from pin 6 of IC-2. Therefore, no DC voltage develops across the cap and meter, so the meter reads 0 center.

When a signal arrives at both RDF antennas at the same time (the antennas are the same distance from the transmitter), the receiver FM detector will have no output since it sees no phase difference in the signal arriving at each antenna.

As soon as the antenna is rotated slightly, the FM detector in the receiver will produce a tone, the frequency of which is determined by the rate at which the antennas are switched. This tone is caused by the signal arriving at one antenna slightly sooner or later than the other. Due to this difference in travel time, it arrives at each antenna with a different phase.

This phase difference comes out of the receiver in the form of positive and negative pulses. See fig. 1(a). When these pulses are fed through the zero-adjust pot to the meter, a DC voltage will develop across the 100 uF capacitor and the meter, and the meter will deflect, say to the left. If we rotate the antennas so the opposite dipole is now closer to the signal source, the pulses out of the receiver now reverse polarity. See fig 1(b). An opposite polarity voltage now develops across the 100 uF cap and meter, so that the meter deflects to the right.

Our circuit is in effect operating as a phase detector. This small DC voltage, developed across the meter, is used to turn on the upper left section of the 339 quad comparator when the meter swings left. When this happens, pin 2 goes low and turns on the upper right section, causing pin 13 to go low and turn on the left, or red, LED. When the antenna is rotated so that the meter swings from left to right, the upper two sections turn off and the lower sections turn on, causing the right, or green, LED to light.

Returning to pin 13 of the 339 for a moment, notice transistor Q4 in the upper right corner. Its base can be connected to pin 13 via the tone shift switch. If S-5 is furned on, whenever pin 13 goes low, indicating a signal to the left, it will turn on Q-4. This transistor serves as an electronic switch; when on, it switches the 0.003 uF capacitor (which is connected to the collector) to the supply bus.

This produces the same effect as connecting the 0.003 uF capacitor across the 0.01 uF cap which is hooked from pin 2 to ground of IC-1. The frequency of the 555 oscillator is lowered, causing the pitch of the tone heard from the speaker to go lower. Therefore, a low tone indicates left and a high tone indicates right. Instead of watching the meter or the LEDs, you can listen to the pitch of the tone.

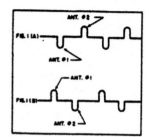

Left: Pulses created by phase difference between the two antennas.

Right and below: Schematics for the RDFing circuit.

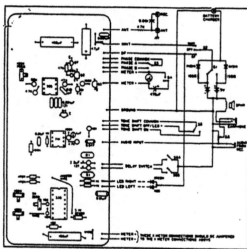

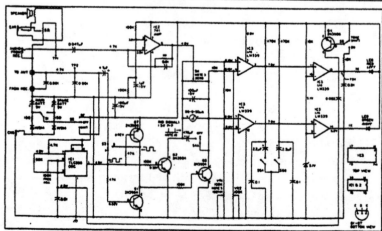

▲

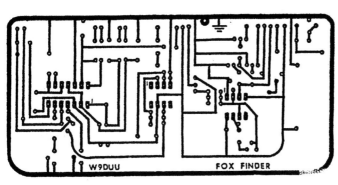

PC board patterns.

Table 1. Parts List

Qty.	Part	RS#			
1	555 timer	276-1718	1	0.047 µF	272-134
1	741 op amp	276-007	2	0.1 µF	272-135
1	LM339	276-1712	1	1 µF 35V tantalum	272-1434
3	2N3904 or equiv.	276-2016	2	2.2 µF 35V tantalum	272-1435
2	2N3906 or equiv.	276-2023	1	4.7 µF 35V elect. axial	272-1012
2	ECG 553 pin diode		2	100 µF 35V elect. axial	272-1028
1	5.1V zener diode	267-565	1	470 µF 16V elect.	272-957
2	1N914 diode	276-1122	1	5k PC mount pot.	271-217
1	red LED	276-041	3	100k miniature pot.	271-284
1	green LED	276-022	1	8Ω stereo fader control	270-047
1	p.c. board	276-168	3	mini SPDT, S-1,S-3,S-5	275-625
1	box (user choice)	270-223	1	mini SPDT (center off), S-2	275-325
2	mini jack	274-247	1	mini SPST, S-4	275-624
1	mini plug	274-286	1	mini DPDT, S-6	275-626
1	coax power jack	274-1565	2	150Ω	271-1312
1	SO-239 jack or BNC	278-201	1	470Ω	271-019
1	2" speaker	40-245	3	1k	271-1321
1	battery snap connector	270-325	4	4.7k	271-1330
1	9V NiCd battery	23-126	4	10k	271-1335
1	9V bat. holder	270-326	2	47k	271-1342
5	0.001 µF	272-126	1	68k	
1	0.003 µF (use 3 of the 0.001 µF caps)		4	100k	271-1347
3	0.01 µF	272-131	2	470K	271-1354
			2	1MΩ	271-1356
			1	50–0–50 uA center zero panel meter	

Note: Meter Sources:
Any center zero meter can be used as long as its in the 50 to 100 microamp deflection range. The Radio
Shack 0–15 volt panel meter can be used by moving the indicator to center position with the position screw.
Also the following two companies have appropriate meters:
A 100–0–100 uA meter (part # MHE 5) is available from Hosfelt Electronics, Inc., 2700 Sunset Blvd.,
Steubenville, OH 43952. Phone: (800) 624–6464.
For a larger meter display you can use the Triplett 320-WS which is available from A.R.E. Surplus, 15272
S.R. 12 E, Findlay, OH 45840. Phone: (419) 422–1558. Blank PC boards are available from the author for
$15 ppd.

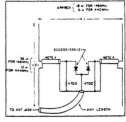

Table 2. Construction Notes

1. Battery voltage = 8 when readings were taken. V on LM339 pins 1, 2, 4, 5, 6, 7, 13 and 14 depends on
   the setting of VR 1 and 2.
2. Battery drain = 7 mA no signal, and about 13 mA with signal applied (L or R LED lit).
3. Antenna and receiver jacks should be counted as close together as possible. Use short leads on the two
   0.001 caps and the 4.7k resistor. Mount the 4.7k resistor at the antenna jack.
4. The length of the coax between the antennas and the switching diodes is not critical, however they
   should be exactly the SAME length.
5. Adjust the zero pot for zero meter reading. Adjust VR 1 and 2 so that the LEDs just extinguish. (No
   signal applied.)
6. With signal aplied, rotate antenna for maximum meter deflection. Adjust the receiver audio level to just
   produce full scale meter deflection.
7. Adjust the oscillator frequency for equal left-right meter deflection with signal applied. Use the highest
   frequency possible. Some radios will have more phase distortion at lower tone frequencies, and can
   even cause the circuit to show reverse direction reading.
8. Use S-4 in the ON position for averaging meter flutter when in high multipath areas, turn S-6 on to store
   LED left or right readings when DFing kerchunckers. Do not turn both S-4 and S-6 on at the same time
   as this will adversely affect your reading. Leave both switches in OFF position for normal DFing.
9. Circuit test: Connect a 1k resistor between TP1 and TP2. Meter and LED should produce a right reading
   with phase switch S-3 in the ON position and a left reading with S-3 in the OFF position.
10. The 8Ω stereo fader control potentiometer is used to control the volume to your earphone or external
    speaker independently of the audio level from your rig into the RDF unit.

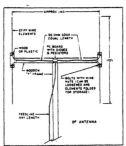

Mechanical mounting details.

▲

Returning to the circuit, the two 2.2 uF capacitors connected to S-6a and S-6b are used as sample and hold capacitors. When S-6 is positioned to ground the negative side of the two caps, they provide a 2-second delay indication of the LED or tone direction reading.

Using the RDF Unit

The phase reversal switch S-3 is used in case you change receivers to a different one which may have the opposite polarity of audio output signal. This has the same effect as having your antenna array backwards—your readings will also be reversed.

Like any other RDF unit, you should practice with the equipment until you become familiar with its operation and using it becomes automatic. There are always enough other things to provide distraction and confusion (multi-path, or reflected signals in particular), and you don't need to add unfamiliarity with your equipment to the list.

A couple of operating hints: If the tone sounds raspy and has high frequency overtones, you probably have some multipath signals. Move your position, if stationary, until the tone sounds pure (no multi-path signals). Take readings at a high elevation and away from reflecting surfaces if possible to minimize multi-path.

It is crucial that the mounting framework for the antenna array be made of non-conducting material; wood or PVC tubing works well. The antennas themselves can be made from telescoping whips, available from sources such as Radio Shack as replacement aerials for portable radios. This allows adjustment of the length of the antennas to suit the frequency of the transmitter in question. A good choice is two pair of dipole TV antennas, or "rabbit ears." The individual elements are usually telescoping affairs mounted on a plastic center block and pivoted so they may be swung back flush to the cross-boom for a more compact package.

Blank circuit boards, populated circuit boards and complete kits with case are available from Paul Bohrer, 1813 Lilac Drive, Indianapolis, IN 46227.

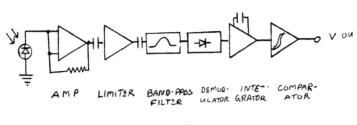

AMP   LIMITER   BAND-PASS   DEMOD-   INTE-   COMPAR-
             FILTER   ULATOR   GRATOR   ATOR

G P 1 U 5 2 X

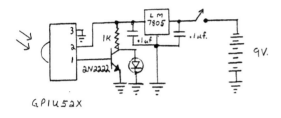

GP1U52X

IR sensor circuitry.

INFRARED SENSOR

A useful device for your tool kit is an infrared sensor (IR sniffer). This item allows you to check the output of remote-control transmitters, passive IR field alarms, and other IR sources, such as may be used in IR surveillance transmitters. An inexpensive unit may be constructed using Radio Shack's JR Detector Module (part number 276-137). At $3.49, this assembly is a real bargain. It contains an IR pick-up diode, amplifier, band-pass filter, integrator, and comparator, all potted up in a metal cube less than one inch on a side. Connecting its output to a driver transistor allows an LED to indicate the presence of pulsed or steady-state IR signals. A nine-volt transistor radio battery is fed to a five-volt regulator integrated

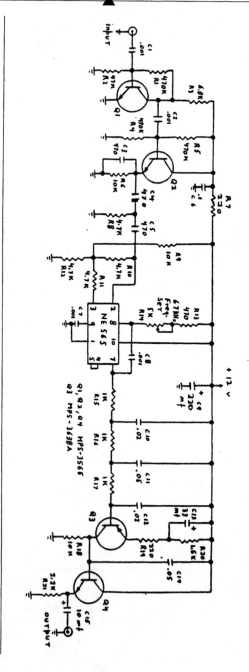

The phone line.

▲

circuit (IC), which supplies the few milliamps of current necessary to operate the circuitry. The driver transistor is noncritical; any garden variety NPN switching transistor will suffice. We use a section of 1" x 2" aluminum stock for a case, but any small opaque box will do, preferably metal.

TELEPHONE VOLTAGE-IMPEDANCE METER

Most telephone sets currently available use modular plugs. To facilitate voltage and resistance readings, a modified volt-ohmmeter (VOM) was developed using a commercial unit manufactured by Micronta and available from Radio Shack (part number 22-171). This is an auto-ranging meter, meaning it will automatically set the range and move the decimal point for the most accurate readout.

Disassemble the case by removing the three small screws from the back cover (one is hidden inside the battery compartment), remove the selector knob (it snaps on and off), lift out the circuit board, and unsolder the red and black test probe wires from the lower left edge of the board.

Take a 12-inch cable with a modular plug on one end and bare wires on the other (Radio Shack part number 279-391 with the spade lugs clipped off; get three when you buy them because you'll need them later) and solder the red lead to the pad where the red test probe was connected, and the green lead to the pad from which you detached the black probe cable.

One more item is necessary: a modular plug Y connector (Radio Shack part number 279-357). With this arrangement, either end of a phone line or the phone itself may be measured during actual operation. Simply unplug the phone from its modular jack, insert the Y connector, and plug the phone into one input of the Y and the meter into the other. Voltage checks may be made for on-hook and off-hook situations, and resistance readings may be made by unplugging the Y from the wall jack.

▲

Two other cables increase the utility of the system. One uses the second modular-plug-to-spade-lug cable you bought. Clip off the spade lugs from the red and green wires and replace them with alligator clips (the black and yellow wires may be cut off flush with the end of the cable). This allows rapid attachment to the connection screws inside a telephone terminal block. A second cable uses a BNC plug on one end and modular plug on the other (the third Radio Shack cable) with the red wire to the center pin of the BNC and the green to ground. This allows for connection to your oscilloscope so you can monitor signals on the line. If your scope uses banana plugs for its input, replace the BNC with a dual male plug. Again, a battery-powered scope is best because of grounding and polarity considerations.

Here is a chart of nominal voltages in a one-line phone system; readings for a line with extension phones will differ unless all phones are off-hook at the same time the readings are taken.

▲

Commercial Equipment and Accessories

SQUELCHED VOX RECORDING

Remote or unattended monitoring and recording of a transmitted signal is usually implemented as shown in the figure below.

At the monitoring site, a scanner or receiver is tuned to the transmitted signal. Because most receivers do not have a tape output, the headphone jack is used. This requires a matching transformer to match the low-impedance output of

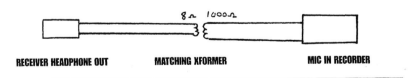

RECEIVER HEADPHONE OUT   MATCHING XFORMER   MIC IN RECORDER

Squelched VOX recording.

▲

the headphone signal to the high-impedance microphone input on the tape recorder. Radio Shack's model 273-1380 audio output transformer works well. The 8-ohm secondary winding is connected to the headphone jack on the receiver and the 1,000-ohm primary winding is plugged into the microphone input of the tape recorder. The squelch level on the receiver is set to mute the background hiss when no signal is being transmitted, and the volume control is set approximately half scale. The VOX level is then set to turn on the recorder when a signal is being received. Some experimentation may be necessary between the volume level and the VOX setting to achieve proper operation. An excellent choice for a recorder is the Sony M-770V microcassette recorder, which records the audio on one track of a stereo microcassette, and the day, date, and time of the recording on the other track (derived from a built-in LCD clock/calendar). This gives a time/date tag of every recording when played back.

MONITOR RECEIVER AND MIXER

When using a monitor receiver for bug hunting, it is usually desirable to wear surround-type headphones to cut down on outside noise and prevent feedback situations. It is also commonplace to equip the rest of the crew with wireless FM mikes and receivers for intercommunication purposes. The receiver operator can mix the audio output of the receiver with the output of his FM communicator. The addition of a momentary push-button switch allows him to cut out the monitor receiver output if there is an incoming message from one of the crew.

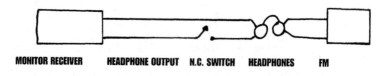

MONITOR RECEIVER   HEADPHONE OUTPUT   N.C. SWITCH   HEADPHONES   FM

Monitor receiver and mixer.

▲

RF ATTENUATORS

Most modern receivers used for transmitter hunting have extremely high-front-end sensitivity. This is great for picking up weak signals, but becomes a problem when you get close to the transmitting source. Front-end overload can cause severe distortion and the signal strength meter is usually at full deflection, making it useless for an indicator of increasing or decreasing distance to the source. If your receiver does not have an RF gain control to decrease the sensitivity of its front end stage, the only solution is an external attenuator or "pad." The cheap and dirty solution involves cable TV attenuators, available in dB increments of 3.0, 4.5, 6.0, 9.0, 12.0, and so on. These devices are usually a cylindrical affair with an F connector on each end. Adaptors can convert to BNC fittings and units can be daisy chained together for higher values. They are inserted in the antenna lead to the receiver and knock down the signal by the rated number of dB. They're cheap and a selection of standard values should be included in your tool box. Most units are good from a few MHz to a GHz or so; check the specs to make sure.

RF SNIFFERS AND PRESCALERS

Active Preselector Model APSi 04; APS204R1 Active Preselector (pat. pend.).

Model APSi 04 is designed for use with a frequency counter such as the model 2600H to dramatically increase the frequency detection distance from a transmitter. The APSi 04 effectively limits the frequency pass band of the counter to 4 MHz. To count, the counter must see a signal that is at least 10 to 15 dB stronger than the background RF level. When the band width is reduced from 3 GHz to 4 MHz, there is an apparent increase in sensitivity (detection range) because of the much smaller amount of background RF.

The pass band of the filter is tuned with the dial on top of the unit to the approximate region of interest. Alternatively, it can be manually swept from 10 MHz to 1 GHz. When used with a signal-level bar-graph-equipped counter such as the 2600H, strong signals can be easily detected from the amount of bar-graph deflection. When used with the POlO computer-based counter, radio receivers such as the ICOM R7000 can be automatically tuned to the frequencies that are detected.

Because the APSi 04 can be battery powered and mounts directly on the back of the 2600H counter, it is ideal for security sweeps, locating stuck transmitters, and picking up radio frequencies from a safe distance.

Model APS2O4R1 is designed for use with a communications receiver. It can be tuned to reject a strong interfering signal close to the desired carrier frequency. Because this unit covers such a wide range of frequencies, one unit can replace several tunable passive filters or a bank of fixed filters. And because the APS204R1 is tuned electronically, there are no mechanical contacts to get dirty or noisy with time.

The features include:

- a new tunable band pass filter system
- 10 MHz to 1,000 MHz range
- continuous tuning over more that five octaves
- maintainance of a constant 4 MHz band width over its entire range
- electronic tuning
- ultimate security sweeper rating.

▲

Typical APSi 04 performance:

Transmitter Type	Counter Only	Counter APSi 04
Cordless Phone	2 feet	120 feet
CB Radio	25 feet	500 feet
VHF Two-Way Radio	80 feet	1/4 to 1/2 mile
Cellular Phone	20 feet	250 feet

Feature	APS204R1	APSi 04
Frequency Range	20-1,000 MHz continuous	10-1,000 MHz continuous
Band Width	4 MHz at -3dB (constant with frequency)	4 MHz at -3dB (constant with frequency)
Ultimate Rejection	60 dB	60 dB
Gain	+3 dB +/- 3 dB	30 dB typical
Noise Figure	10 dB max	N/A
Third order output intercept point	+15 dBm typical	N/A
Size (HxWxL)	1.5" x 4" x 7"	1.5" x 4" x 7"
Power requirements	13 to 15 VOC 400mA typical	18 volts (two 9v transistor radio batteries)

Band Pass Filter/Amplifier Model CF800

Model CF800 (820-870 MHz) is a frequency counter accessory used with model 2600H Handi-Counter that extends range for cellular frequency finding. This counter works by boosting desired RE signals while eliminating unwanted portions of RE spectrum.

▲

The features include:

- MMIC amplifier followed by a 5 pole bandpass filter
- 9-volt Ni-Cad battery power housed in an extruded aluminum cabinet that can attach to the 2600H or 3000 Handi-Counters (TM) for full portable operation
- while it can be used with any frequency counter that has good sensitivity in the 820 through 870 frequency range, the signal strength bar graph feature of the above mentioned models is extremely useful when frequency finding.

Specifications:

- typical distance from a 600 mW transmitter increases from 20 feet to more than 200 feet (distances may vary as a function of in-band background RE level)
- gain in excess of 20 dB; filter section specifications remain proprietary at this time
- dimensions are 7" high x 3.9" wide x 1.4" deep
- weight is 12 oz.
- connector type is BNC
- antenna is model RD800

Techniques in Counter-Surveillance

SPECIFICATIONS	APS2O4R1	APS1O4
Frequency Range	20-1000 MHz continuous	10-1000 MHz continuous
Band width	4 MHz at -3dB, constant with frequency	4 MHz at -3dB, constant with frequency
Ultimate rejection	60 dB	60 dB
Gain	+3 dB +/- 3 dB	30 dB typical
Noise Figure	10 dB max	N/A
Third order output intercept point	+15 dBm typical	N/A
Size(HxWxL)	1.5" x 4' x 7"	1 .5" x 4" x 7"
Power requirements	13 to 15 VOC, 400mA typical	18 volts (two 9v transistor radio batteries)

Band Pass Filter/Amplifier.

Model CF800

Model CF800 (820 - 870MHz) is a frequency counter accessory used with model 2600H HANDl-COUNTER that extends range for Cellular Frequency Finding. This counter works by boosting desired RE signals while eliminating unwanted portion of RE spectrum.

FEATURES:
• MMIC amplifier followed by a 5 pole bandpass filter.
• 9 Volt NiCad battery powered.
• Housed in an extruded aluminum cabinet that can attach to the 2600H or 3000 Handi-Counters(TM) for full portable operation.
• While it can be used with any frequency counter that has good sensitivity in the 820 through 870 frequency range, the signal strength bar graph feature of the above mentioned models is extremely useful when frequency finding.

SPECIFICATIONS:

Typical Distance: From a 600 mW transmitter increases from 20 feet to over 200 feet (Distances may vary as a function of in-band back ground RE level).
Gain: In excess of 20 dB. Filter section specifications remain proprietary at this time.
Size: 7" high x 3.9' wide x 1.4" deep. **Weight:** 12 oz.
Connector type: BNC
Antenna: Model RD800

Model CF800 band pass filter/amplifier.

BATTERY TYPES AND CAPACITIES

Alkaline

Size	Rated Drain (ma.)	Load (ohms)	Capacity (hrs.)
AAA	25	50	28
AA	130	10	12
C	300	4	12
D	320	4	30

Industrial Ni-Cad

Size	Capacity (amp-hours)
AA	0.5
A	0.6
Sub-C	1.2
C	1.8
1/2 D	2.2
D	4.0

PRIMARY BATTERIES

Primary batteries are nonrechargeable; you use them until they die and then throw them away. There are five common types available:

- standard
- heavy duty

▲

- alkaline cells based on zinc-carbon construction
- mercury cells based on zinc-carbon construction
- lithium.

Of the three zinc-carbon types, heavy-duty cells have approximately twice the capacity of standard types, and alkaline cells can have three to six times the amp-hour rating of a standard unit. Alkaline cells also maintain rated output voltage much better into continuous-duty high-current loads. Despite their higher cost, they should be the only choice for critical applications, especially those where replacement is difficult or impossible. These cells also have excellent shelf life, maintaining their capacity for long periods in standby situations.

Mercury cells have a very stable output voltage (generally 1.35 to 1.4 volts per cell) and excellent shelf life. They maintain rated output voltage even at relatively high-load demands, but are somewhat limited in overall capacity. They are typically used in low-power transmitters and similar equipment where current drain is low. A major advantage is their small size; many of the FM transmitters use one or two cells about the size of an aspirin tablet.

Lithium batteries are available in the same standard sizes as zinc-carbon cells. They have very high amp-hour ratings, but many of the over-the-counter consumer types do not handle heavy current demands gracefully. Some of the newer chemistries, such as the lithium thionyl-chloride types, overcome this limitation, but they are usually only available in industrial-grade cells.

If you have a crucial application where battery life is a major consideration, such as a remote transmitter or an unattended tape recorder or monitor, the best approach is to choose the best battery available and do a life test in advance of its intended use. Knowing how long a given device will function before it dies from exhausted batteries can prevent disastrous situations and the loss of crucial data.

▲

SECONDARY BATTERIES

Secondary cells are those that can be recharged multiple times. The most common types are nickel cadmium (Ni-Cads) and lead-acid configurations (Gel-Cells) in which the electrolyte is a viscous compound that allows operation with the cell on its side or when inverted. Like lithium cells, Ni-Cads are available in consumer and commercial versions, with the commercial units having considerably greater capacity than their consumer counterparts. Ni-Cads tolerate heavy current demands nicely, but have noticeably lower amp-hour capacity than an equivalently sized alkaline cell. They tend to lose their charge during prolonged storage and tend to exhibit memory characteristics if not discharged completely before recharging. As a result, they are rarely used in remote or inaccessible applications because it's quicker and easier to replace an alkaline battery with its attendant longer life than to recharge a Ni-Cad in the field. They are quite useful for portable test and monitoring equipment however, especially if precharged replacement sets are available.

Gel-Cells are even more popular for portable equipment. They are available in a wide variety of sizes with capacities ranging from several hundred milliamp-hours to many amp-hours. Because recharge times can be considerable for the larger units, spare, charged-up batteries that can be quickly substituted are desirable.

Several exceptions exist regarding the caveat against using rechargeable batteries for remote transmitting applications. In the case of high-powered phone bugs, the excessive current demands when transmitting can load down the voltages present on telephone lines, making detection much easier. As a result, battery-operated VOX transmitters are often employed. If the battery is a rechargeable type, a simple trickle charger can be employed across the phone line voltage, recharging the battery at a much lower current drain during periods of nontransmission, greatly reducing

▲

the voltage drop, and eliminating the need to replace the battery periodically.

Transmitters and monitoring sites placed outdoors can use a solar panel to recharge batteries during daylight hours. This technique is used extensively by the highway department to keep battery operated emergency roadside call boxes in operation. Solar panels can be had in many voltage and size configurations, often at reduced prices from surplus catalogs.

Several other battery configurations bear mentioning. Panasonic manufactures a line of cells under the trade name Myact, which are two-volt rechargeable cells approximately 1/4" thick, 1" wide, and 2" to 3" long, with capacities ranging from 500 milliamp hours to 1.6 amp-hours. They may be series connected to arrive at any multiple of two volts, and their thin profile allows great latitude in tight spaces.

There has also been a great deal of interest in the new Polaroid 6-volt battery designed for their camera's film packs. While not rechargeable, it measures approximately 3" x 4" with a thickness of less than 1/8". This allows for some truly creative placements—inside picture frames and under carpets are two examples where standard batteries would be a problem.

▲

Charts and Waveforms

FREQUENCY ALLOCATION CHART

550-1,600	kH	AM Broadcast Band
29-43	MHz	Government, Fire, Business, Police
43-44	MHz	Telephone Maintenance, Paging, Emergency
44-50	MHz	Police, Fire, Local and Federal Governent
50-54	MHz	Amateur Six-Meter Band
54-72	MHz	TV Channels 2, 3, and 4
76-88	MHz	TV Channels 5 and 6
88-108	MHz	FM Commercial Broadcast
108-136	MHz	Aircraft Navigation, Air Traffic Control
136-144	MHz	Federal Government
144-148	MHz	Amateur Two-Meter Band
148-150	MHz	Federal Government
150-151	MHz	Tow Trucks, Highway Maintenance
151-153	MHz	Business, Paging, Taxi

153-156	MHz	Power, Fire, Local Government, Police, Emergency
156-157	MHz	Marine
157-158	MHz	Paging, Auto Clubs, Taxi, Mobile Phones
158-161	MHz	Paging, Forestry, Police, Highway, Trucking, ER
161-162	MHz	Marine, Marine Phone
162-174	MHz	Federal Government
174-216	MHz	TV Channels 7-13
216-220	MHz	Telemetry
220-225	MHz	Amateur Radio
225-400	MHz	Military, Aircraft, Federal Government
400-406	MHz	Satellite
406-420	MHz	Federal Government
420-450	MHz	Amateur Radio
452-453	MHz	Taxi, Trucking, Auto Club, Automobile Roadside
453-454	MHz	Police, Fire, Highway
454-455	MHz	Mobile Phone
460-460	MHz	Police, Fire Repeater Transmitters
460-462	MHz	Business, Taxi
462-462	MHz	CE
463-465	MHz	Emergency
456-470	MHz	Mobile Units
470-806	MHz	UHF TV Channels
806-821	MHz	Mobile Phone
821-825	MHz	Phone Satellite Uplink
825-866	MHz	Cellular, Mobile Phones
866-870	MHz	Phone Satellite Downlink
870-896	MHz	Cellular Phones
896-902	MHz	Business Radio
902-928	MHz	Industrial, Scientific, Medical, Amateur Radio

▲

AM-FM PULSE MODULATION

In amplitude modulation, the carrier signal has its amplitude modulated in proportion to the message bearing (lower frequency) signal. The magnitude of it is chosen to be less than or equal to one because of demodulation, i.e., recovery of the signal from the received signal.

The frequency of the modulating signal is chosen to be much smaller than that of the carrier signal. Try to think of what would happen if the modulating index were bigger than one.

Think of how you might demodulate this signal, which means to recover the signal from the modulated signal. The AM stations on your radio go from 550 kHz to 1610 kHz. The maximum frequency that is transmitted is usually no more than 15 kHz. The bandwidth of an AM scheme, which is the amount of space that it occupies in the Fourier domain, is twice that of the modulating signal.

One version of AM is called double side band AM (DSBAM) because we send signals on both sides of the wave. It is more efficient to transmit only one of the side bands (so-called single side band AM; USBAM and LSBAM for upper and lower side bands, respectively), or if the filtering requirements for this are too arduous to send, a part of one of the side bands. This is what is done in commercial analog NTSC television, which is known as vestigial side band AM. The TV video signal has a bandwidth of about 4.25 MHz, but only 1 MHz of the lower side band of the signal is transmitted. The FCC allocates 6 MHz per channel (thus 0.75 MHz is left for the sound signal, which is an FM signal; see the next section).

You may have wondered how we can listen to AM radio channels on both stereo and mono receivers. The trick that is used to generate a modulating signal by adding a DSB version (carrier at 38 kHz suppressed) version of the output of the difference between the left and right channels added to the sum of the left and right channels unmodulated. The resulting modulating signal has a bandwidth of about 60 kHz. A mono

▲

receiver gets the sum signal, whereas a stereo receiver separates out the difference as well and reconstitutes the left and right channel outputs.

FREQUENCY MODULATION

FM is a so-called angle modulation scheme that was inspired by phase modulation but has proved to be more useful partly for its ease of generation and decoding. The main advantages of FM over AM are:

- improved signal-to-noise ratio (about 25dB) with regard to man-made interference
- smaller geographical interference between neighboring stations
- less radiated power
- well-defined service areas for given transmitter power.

The disadvantages of FM are:

- much more bandwidth (as much as 20 times as much)
- more complicated receiver and transmitter.

In this scheme, the frequency of the modulating signal is changed in proportion to the message signal. Here the signal is assumed to be normalized so that the maximum of the integral is one and is called the frequency deviation of the modulation scheme. Figure FM1 is an example of what FM signals look like.

Your FM dial goes from 88 MHz to 108 MHz (this range is between the frequency ranges for TV channels 1 through 6 and 7 through 12). For a typical radio station there is some leeway allowed, which varies from about 150 at low frequencies (50 Hz or so) to 3.75 at high frequencies (20 kHz or so), and a very rough bandwidth figure is 200 kHz. Thus, KDFC 102.5 on your FM dial goes from 102.4 MHz to 102.6 MHz.

▲

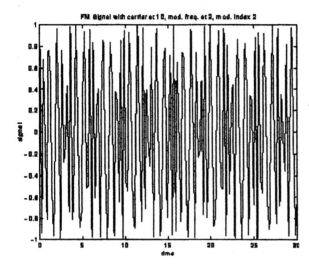

FM Signal with carrier at 1 0, mod. freq. at 2, mod. index 2

FM modulation with modulating frequency 1.

Try to puzzle over how you might try to demodulate FM. (Think differentiation!)

PULSE MODULATION SCHEMES

Here the basic idea is to use a pulse train as the carrier signal. The choice of this pulse train can be quite interesting from the standpoint of energy and spectral content consumption. One can use square pulses, raised cosine pulses, or sync function (Nyquist) pulses. For simplicity, let's talk about square pulse trains.

The characteristics of the pulse train that can be varied are its amplitude, width, and position of the leading edge. We will talk about the first two ideas.

The modulation schemes that do this are called pulse amplitude modulation (PAM) and pulse width modulation (PWM) respectively. The figure on page 110 shows what is known as a passband PAM, in that the PAM pulse train is actually also multiplied by a carrier frequency sinusoid to enable transmission at a higher frequency.

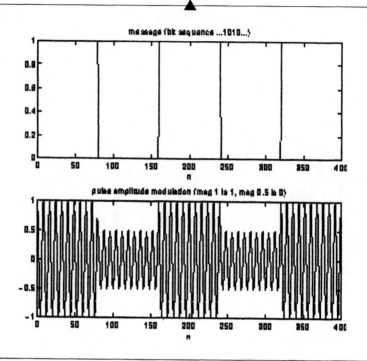

Passband PAM modulation

Note that this basic scheme can be made more sophisticated by using several amplitude levels. For example, one can group the bits into groups of 2, i.e., 00, 01, 10, and 11, and have four different amplitude levels for each of these groups. This is referred to as quadrature pulse amplitude modulation (QPAM or QAM for short). QAM actually is used for alphabets of size other than four. For example, 2,400 baud full duplex modems use 16 QAM (corresponding to grouping four bits together). 9,600 baud; 14,400 baud; and 28,800 baud modems use 32 QAM, 128 QAM, and 1024 QAM respectively (along with something known as trellis coding, which introduces redundancy by doubling the number of signal points in the QAM configuration). PWM is illustrated in the figure on page 111. The circuitry required to generate this is complicat-

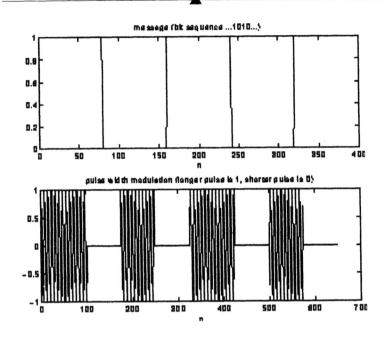

Pulse width modulation.

ed, but it is extremely conceptually important because there is good reason to believe that neurons transmit information using PWM spike trains.

60 HZ AC MODULATION

It is possible to mic a room and impress the audio information on the 60-cycle AC power wiring, and then retrieve it from any other AC outlet in the same building. This is the principle behind wireless intercoms; the audio information modulates the 60 Hz waveform and is available at any outlet common to the same power wiring. Plugging a battery-operated oscilloscope across the AC line will reveal a waveform similar to these.

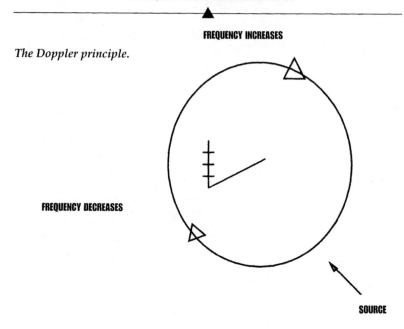

The Doppler principle.

DOPPLER SYSTEMS

Most of the RDF units and vehicle tracking systems operate on some variation of the Doppler principle. To visualize how this system works, imagine an antenna rotating at the end of an arm. As the antenna moves toward the transmitting source, the frequency of the received signal appears to increase. As the antenna recedes from the source, the apparent frequency tends to decrease.

In practice, two or four antennas are used in a fixed array and the receiver is switched from one to the next at a rapid rate.

ANTENNAS AND WAVELENGTH FORMULAS

The standard antenna for monitoring and tracking receivers is a telescoping whip 18 to 30 inches long when fully extended. This works well with moderate to weak signals and is sensitive for 360 degrees, i.e., it is an omnidirectional device.

When approaching the transmitting source, the antenna may be partially or fully collapsed, thus lowering its sensitivity and preventing receiver overload. However, being nondirectional, its only indication of the direction of the source is an increase in signal strength as the source is approached. Directional antennas such as yagi and log periodic arrays, which look like the familiar multi-element TV antenna, are directional and have a capture area of 30 to 90 degrees relative to the front of the array. This allows pinpointing the location of the source more easily. Additionally, these antennas have two or three times the gain of a simple vertical whip. Unfortunately, they respond most effectively only to a rather limited range of frequencies.

If you're only interested in a specific frequency band, a directional array works well, but there is virtually no antenna available that will cover the extremely wide range of frequencies that need to be covered in a comprehensive sweep. One good compromise is a set of TV rabbit ears—two telescoping whips with a common base. When extended in a straight line, they form a half-wave dipole array whose maximum sensitivity is on a line perpendicular to their common length. As the frequency increases, they can be partially collapsed to better match the frequency of interest. The formula for the length of a half-wave array is shown here.

$$\text{FREQUENCY HALF-WAVE} \ = \ \frac{5905}{\text{FREQUENCY IN MHz}} \ \text{INCHES}$$

If using a whip or dipole for transmitter hunting, polarization effects must be considered. If the transmitter antenna is in a vertical plane, the receiver antenna will capture more signal if it is also vertical, and considerably less if it is at right angles to the source antenna. The same is true if the source uses a horizontal polarization.

When close to the source, the signal will be so strong that antenna matching is unimportant; collapsing the antenna or adding attenuation will be more important to reduce the chance of receiver overload.

One last useful trick when using an omnidirectional whip on a tracking receiver or RF sniffer. Holding the receiver or sniffer low and close to your body so that your body forms a shield to the incoming signal if it is between it and the receiving antenna allows you to turn through a 360-degree circle and note the change in signal strength. The strongest reading will occur when you are facing the source with your body behind the receiving antenna.

VIDEO WAVEFORMS

A typical television signal is comprised of several parts including:

- a luminance portion (which contains the video information and timing signals)
- a color-burst component (which holds the color information)
- a sound subcarrier (which represents the audio signal)

Video is transmitted as an AM signal, whereas the sound is FM. The important thing to notice in the diagram is the relatively wide bandwidth occupied by the complete waveform (typically 6 MHz). Allowing a slight dead space on each side results in a bandwidth of 8 MHz. This is why most amateur TV transmission is done at higher frequencies, such as 450 MHz and 902 MHz, where there is less signal density than at lower frequencies. In the 902-928 MHz amateur and industrial band, the total spectrum of 26 MHz allows three channels of 8 MHz bandwidth to operate simultaneously.

Consumer video transmitter-receiver combinations used to transmit a VCR signal to another room of your house operate at low power (legal under part 15 of the FCC regulations). Units such as the Gemini Rabbit have a three-channel switch on the transmitter. This unit has become quite popular with surveillance types; it's relatively inexpensive, can be converted to 12-volt operation, and has a range of 100 feet or so. At the TV receiver end, a down-converter unit takes the 902 MHz signal and heterodynes it down to around 50 to 70 MHz so it can be tuned in as a channel 2, 3, or 4 signal. With the proliferation of small, cheap CCD cameras, an audio-video surveillance system is quite easy to implement. This band bears particular attention during a sweep procedure.

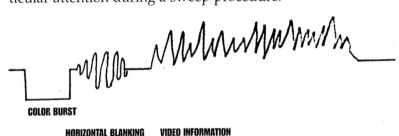

COLOR BURST

HORIZONTAL BLANKING   **VIDEO INFORMATION**

One line of NTSC standard color video.

DECIBEL FORMULAS AND TABLES

The decibel, abbreviated dB, is an often misunderstood term denoting the ratio between two power levels or two voltage levels. The formula is,

$$N(dB) = 10 \log (P2 / P1)$$

where P1 and P2 are the power ratios being compared. If both power levels are developed across equal impedances, the corresponding voltage ratios may be used.

$$N(dB) = 20 \log (V2/V1)$$

These values are meaningless unless a reference level is stated, i.e., voltage 2 is so many dB higher than voltage 1. The terms dBm and dBw are often used to refer to decibel levels with respect to 1 milliwatt and 1 watt respectively. A power level of 1 milliwatt into 600 ohms is a standard and is referred to as 0 dBm, which corresponds to .775 volts. 0 dBm into a 50-ohm resistance corresponds to .225 volts.

Levels above or below these figures are specified as + or - dBm and refer to a specific voltage or current, not a ratio. Below is a partial table of decibel levels and the corresponding voltage and power ratios.

Voltage Ratio	Power Ratio	- dB +	Voltage Ratio	Power Ratio
1.000	1.000	0.0	1.000	1.000
0.891	0.794	1.0	1.122	1.259
0.708	0.501	3.0	1.413	1.995
0.501	0.251	6.0	1.995	3.981
0.316	0.100	10.0	3.162	10.000
0.100	0.010	20.0	10.000	100.000

Useful figures to remember are +3 dB is double the power, -3 dB is one-half the power, +6 dB is four times the power, -6 dB is 1/4 the power, 10 dB is 10 times the power, 20 dB is 100 times the power (10^2), 30 dB is 1,000 times the power (10^3), and so on.